A New Philosophical Classic:
THEORY OF LOVE

A New Philosophical Classic:
THEORY OF LOVE

Sankar Sarkar

PARTRIDGE
A Penguin Random House Company

To order additional copies of this book, contact
Partridge India
000 800 10062 62
www.partridgepublishing.com/india
orders.india@partridgepublishing.com

CONTENTS

DEDICATION

To my loving Mother

PREFACE

With a jaunty proclivity I am writing the preface of 'A New Philosophical Classic: Theory of love' with a new innovative concept. Really I am glad of getting republished again this book with Partridge Publishing. I've endeavoured my best to make the subject matter of this book more presentable and suitable amid a few additions keeping an eye on the interest of the advanced dynamic world. The theme and thought is elucidated in assorted abiding aspects how love has upheld the mystery of creation concerning both life and world. The exquisite impulses are associated with inventive ideas and views in philosophical approaches based on the classic panoramic outlooks. Having related to the unique tunc of universe both empirical and idealistic vistas have prevailed over the hackneyed perspectives in this book. The different thoughts and feelings synchronize with an artistic notion. Here love deserves the innermost reinforcement in life as an underlying force, and it also exists even in every atom and molecule of everything as causal attractive force to keep the whole creation in motion. I don't know whether my ' A New Philosophical Classic: Theory of love' will be able to occupy a little corner in the heart of my readers regarding their disquiet life. I shall feel joy if this book can assuage the least burden of the irksome and monotonous life and lull them to sleep by the whispering of the tale of love into their ears. My readers will know when they will read this book how I have made a cordial effort to be a fond lover to them to mitigate their unuttered exhaustion coming in contact with the closest of their fatigued mind. Besides, I greet them to realize how I had been cherishing such feelings in my heart to share with them. Before concluding I intend to offer my heartfelt gratitude and altruistic appreciation to the Partridge, A Penguin Random House Company, and again I desire to tell my readers that life is sweet so long as love exists.

October 2013   Author

A FEW WORDS: WHY WOULD YOU READ THIS BOOK?

Whatever visible is relative not everlasting:

Whatever invisible is abstract but everlasting.

The co-existence of life, world and philosophy

Is nothing but God's analytical love therapy.

I greet my readers with a handful of love and request them to listen patiently to what I intend to tell. I desire to speak of love` which empowers you inwardly to carry on your life to its ultimate destination amid the continuous struggles. I don't have any wish to fritter away your precious time telling a life story of an unknown flower, however beautiful, of an unknown dreamy land, nor a description of the unuttered words of a pair of blue eyes of a lovely princess far away, nor a wailing for an unrequited love of a prince, nor a long heart-touching missive drenched with emotion. This world is like a wonderful labyrinth, and every living being is its 'mystery', but human life is more mysterious than that. Despite what the most mysterious power it is by which this vast creation is lively and speedy. And it has also kept both the animate and the inanimate closely related, as if, in a divine ecstatic way. What is it? It is nothing but love which is the invisible purified power resulting from the mélange of each specific subtle force and energy of eight elements (i.e. five of them are visible viz soil, water, fire, air and space, and three of them invisible viz mind, understanding (intelligence) and vanity) which have coalesced in human body, that is nonexistent without these elements. Even this vast universe exists in the presence of the unseen force and power of the five invisible elements. Each of them consists of the endless unseen attractive force or power. Hence every living being is truly existed under the influence of the purified power of 'love', but human life is superior to the others for the dominance of the three inner elements. So 'love' is an eternal hunger in human life; if not, life would not be existent. That 'love is a purified power' has been manifested in this book from different angles of outlook in the midst of considerable number of definitions, discussions and instances. It has been endeavoured best to unveil its main purport to the readers through theorization of the expected subject matter how love (i.e. purified power) has influenced the human life at its every turn. Its scope is so wide and panoramic from which no man can escape. Here it has been also expounded how a man can avert himself from the indecent path amid moralizing and enhancing the morale for contending with this ill fate inspired by love. This book also treats how 'love' has come in to being regarding human body. Besides, the approach of the book is to make the people realize and be conscious of 'love' that is beatific power which provides a man with necessary inner media to confront any dilemma and can embrace a tension free and happy life in his precarious prolonged journey. After all, having applied this power (i.e. love) a man must be able to dispel all bitterness from his life. I believe this book is necessary for every man to excel his acerbic step in his daily life in this decadent society. Finally 'love' is the purified name of the purified power which unveils itself through every life irrespective of caste and creed, the rich and the poor. Having conquered the untruthful power it ushers in peace in life. Hence 'love' is commendable and laudable, beautiful and sweet, sacred and eternal power and eternal power. So life is a slave to love, and both life and the world are nothing but the shadow of love (i.e. purified power). Everything is replete with love, because without power or energy nothing seems to be existent. As a result all yearn after 'Love'.

WHY I INTEND TO WRITE THIS BOOK

A fervent longing has impelled me to hold the pen to think of writing this book. I have found it difficult to start this book because of several obstacles whenever I make up my mind to begin. I was not able to write a single word and arrange conspicuously the thought of my subject. The hidden sufferings, unuttered agonies of the hearts, sorrows, antipathies, indignations and heart-rending cries choke my voice to utter any word with my pen. So the unuttered and suppressed agony of the thousand people of this decadent society have coerced me to catch hold of my pen to write a few words for ushering in a little peace in life. I know that it is quite impossible for me to participate in such a great work yet it is my keen effort and endeavour for reaching your heart, I don't know whether I'll be able or not.

My two poor eyes have melted with tears, which I cannot prevent from surging. I am a discordant tune in this melodious vastness. So, in spite of wishing, I have no capacity to gratify you with my broken tune of my writing. yet I have self-confidence. I am a man. I am not out of this vast family. With this self-confidence I dare to stretch out my friendly hand towards you, because I am also a member of this family. I believe that you will never ostracize me from this family to which you and I still belong. If you ask me how I have written this book! How I have floated in the stream of thought of perturbation. I have confronted different colourful incidents and events. Many of them have touched my heart and aroused my consciousness. And my memory is stuffed with such bitter experiences. I have observed how the fires of frustration, hopelessness, despondency and dissimilarity have burnt both in society and family, even it touches man's personal life. This book is for any class of people irrespective of caste and creed. I have amassed many bitter experiences and ordeals through sundry incidents in every step of my active life. It is such an unspoken and unseen agony that eats into the very essence of our life; even not only the personal life but the whole world of life facing this unuttered quandary by which influence we are getting weak both mental and physical aspects. As a result, we are still on decaying. It is a matter of astonishment that how humanity is selling at the rate of waste paper in the market of universe.

Now a day the human society is on the wane. Every life has become restless, indignant, and also acrimonious because of losing its pleasure. Besides, man is becoming hostile and harmful to one another. Day-after-day people are going to be contentious. Why? Every life is swinging under the influence of frustration and hopelessness. Most people in every family, as if they are suffering from something uncanny. They look gloomy and depressed. In course of my life, I have come across many men among the lower class, the middle class and the upper class, and most of them feel dispirited mentally.

It is seen that those who are rich and well to do are not suffering from any want of money. in spite of enough riches and wealth they look unhappy. Why? Even they are not able to get a sound sleep at night. They have to take sleeping pill. Truly speaking, they seem to be happy outwardly. No family is free from such strained and suppressed conflict, they seem healthy and aglow, but they are frail in respect of confronting any battle or struggle of life. Why? When I have cast my two tearful eyes upon the young generation, I feel stunned. how they are decaying themselves and have strayed away from the path of the truth. Emptiness engulfs the young generation. It seems that they have contracted with an unseen and incurable malady that makes them enervated to go ahead of facing and struggling all types of impasses in this path. Such unspoken agony saddens me. I don't know what little I shall be able to satisfy you.

They are too weak mentally to brood properly over doing any arduous task. Thus I have noticed that thousands of people are smoldering in the deficiency of the food of mind regardless of all classes of people. It seems they have lost something. They look criminal. As if, they have done some sinful act. Many people desire to commit suicide. they are compelled to relinquish their all hopes defeated by life's struggle. Why? Despite immense wants, what type of necessity it is! it is such a want, which affects every personal life and family life. They are faltering due to lack of a little peace and happiness. Where have these gone? Such disappointment even extends its dark hand directly towards the social and national life.

Almost every life and every family is suffering from a lack of tranquility. A sort of suppressed agony is disconcerting them. It is very much difficult to speak a word of peace being a representative of this decadent society. Yet I dare to stretch out my friendly hand towards you. My friends! My readers! I don't know whether my writing could touch your agonized heart or not. I have a little belief in my perturbative mind to awaken your trance. It is my friendly request to go through this book. Perhaps, you may get the answer of your unspoken question of your mind. Though you are not needy, or you have no financial want, yet you feel somewhat want that makes your life restless and miserable. Such want debilitates you. Even you are losing your own balance to keep pace with the other members of your family, friends and relatives. In spite of working hard you are not able to establish a little tranquility or peace of mind in the members of your family. Your family seems to be immersing into a constant state of disturbance. Why? Not only you but also the whole world feels this want. It does not restrict to a personal life, even it spreads everywhere. We are too modern and sophisticated to appreciate that 'Love' of which want can make you a destitute, a weak and a forlorn person. Its presence in your life makes you a real happy man and can bring true peace and serenity in every sphere of your life! How? And how may you get at its golden contact? How will you enhance your latent essence relating to the worth of yourself? Have you enquired of your own essence?

Have you discerned how morality has been banished from your life like a dripping leaf and decadence of humanity is going onward? In spite of ever wakefulness, how people are pretending to be unaware of the true state of affairs. They don't hesitate to put forward the pretext of sleeping, despite being awakened fully. Is it love? In the name of love thousands of blooming lives are being destroyed, is it love? With whom you have built up a beautiful dreamy hut, No sooner had a year finished than it got dilapidated in the absence of any strong gust. But it gets extirpated by only the storm of your strained mind and misunderstanding. Is it called love? How thousands of bondage of relation is breaching day-after-day in every step of life? What sort of love it is! It can't leave the miles of road behind and move towards facing obstacles to a fixed destination! Is it love? A deep and a long sigh of frustration of inhumanity overcast the sky of humanity. The whole nation is still getting immersed in the depth of oblivion.

I never long for praise and lots of congratulation from you. Only my destitute heart will go on bestowing its thanks upon your friendly attempt for stretching out your hands towards me. I am very glad of you, because you have sacrificed a few minutes to listen to the whisper of my agonized pen. My effort and endeavour will be successful, however little, if my any word or the words, or any sentence or the sentences or any thought can bring a ray of hope of peace in your tormented life; or if you are able to solve any predicament in your life with the help of my writing or if my book can bring a little leisure in the world of your pensive mood in your restless life. I earnestly request you not to take me from your scornful corner of outlook of your life. I want all of you a peaceful life. I pray to God to shower His auspicious blessing upon you and remove the thorns of distress from the path of your life. Let your life be simple, and simplicity is your first manner. Let Truth be an inspiration in your life, and knowledge is your measuring stick regarding beauty and consciousness, and love is your source of all energy and power in course of your life. Perhaps, I am not able to drench your mind with the sweetness of my writing. I am not apposite for immortalizing you with the subterranean flow of the sweet nectar of my thought. I am merely a man. So, I don't know whether you will take my writing heartily or bitterly. I request all of you to test my writing regarding your life. per chance, it may rouse you from the state of trance. Even this book may impart you with a handful of pleasure to forget all sufferings from your life.

O' my friends! You are asked to be calm and quiet and go patiently through ten pages of this book. I believe that this book will wake you up from a state of disquiet and must help you like a friend in the world of ignorance. I hope it may also usher in spring of tranquility in your disturbed mind. If not, you stop reading further and forget it forever. Even you may throw this book in the dust; I hope it will be your real return to me. I'll accept it gladly.

WHY I'VE PREFERRED THIS SUBJECT MATTER

Love is a sublime art, but life is a living art. Love becomes lively whenever it comes in contact with life. So, it is very arduous to explicit in a few words why I have preferred this subject. I don't know what little I shall be able to satisfy you with my thoughts. Yet I am endeavoring my best to discuss it keeping an eye on the subject matter. In this respect, if you help me with your amicable inspiration, it will be very facile task for me to express its purport to you. I have a good faith and confidence in your altruistic desire and will regarding my writing. So, I think that I'll be successful in making you understand about my discussion. Before discussing this expected matter I intend to say you that whatever seems to be true cannot be seen with external eyes, only they are felt by perceptible organs. Suppose, if you are asked-have you seen 'mind'? Or 'soul? Or 'heart'? What will you give answer? Just like it, my selected subject matter is 'Love' that is an unseen attractive force or energy or power, which beautifies every flower-like human life.

As we charm at the beauty of flowers of a garland, but we never think how this beauty has come into being. How these flowers have been strung together, and arranged properly, and which attractive force has enabled these flowers to keep themselves sequential. Only we are so overwhelmed with outward beauty but we are not conscious and aware of its true recondite reason for which such external beauty is possible. Here, have we ever thought of that thread of the garland? Remaining unseen this 'thread' has put all flowers in order in the garland. Like an unseen 'thread' "love" has kept also all lives like flowers in a garland of the mankind. But, we are totally unaware of this surreptitious matter relating to our life. If the 'thread' of a garland is cut off, all flowers of this garland will get scattered; and then the garland loses its true beauty. if it is, whenever thread like 'love' (i.e. attraction) is cut off, every life like flower of the garland of the whole of mankind will get fallen off. Perhaps, you have realized my point of discussion. We have become so emotional and crazy for our selfishness without taking care of sustaining this 'love' like energy or attraction to be kept permanently.

So, we are not cognizant of and attentive to uphold and elevate this unseen attractive energy in our life. As a result, we are getting enervated day-after-day though we are getting flesh in our body. We are still on the threshold of decadence. It is conspicuous that we are forgetting to evaluate the worth of love like energy. Today we are offering an oblation at the feet of the distorted image of love having forgotten the true deity of love. You are feeling its unwholesome consequence from your personal life to social life. So, I welcome all of you to enhance that love in your life to become energetic and enthusiastic with this love-like energy and to defeat all inauspicious power, and enjoy real peace in your life. I intend to speak of love, which is the only 'thing' that can impart a heavenly and pleasant life. So, if you long for a happy life you must learn to revolutionize love in your mind. Otherwise, it will be truly impossible to save your personal life from a deadly deterioration in the arena of humanity.

Don't forget my readers! The entire nations of human being are just like a garland. Every man is like a flower, which is put in an order in this garland. So, there is so attraction from heart to heart; but by which attractive force we are so close to one another in this vast garland. So, we have to suffer from the separation, dismemberment and disintegration in every turn of life until we become a worshipper or devotee to the true deity of love like energy.

If you want to surmount any quandary throughout your life you have no any other way without yielding to this supreme power of 'love'. if you think deeply it will be clear that maximum problematic issue arises from the matter of mind. In a wider sense, this is love that can only solve our all sort of problems amid proper applications. So, I want 'love'. I yearn after 'love". I long for 'love'. I want everyone to cherish it in his mind to get a peaceful and felicitated life.

Before I have discussed that every life is like a beautiful flower. You see that we have an intense affection for a flower for its beauty and sweet smell that enrapture our organs of perception; even it gradually awakens the other organs of our body. So every flower exists with some true qualities, even every other thing also has some distinctive qualities. But here I have taken a flower as a paradigm regarding life. You never forget that everything is vested with somewhat beauty that may vary from person to person. However, a life is just like a beautiful flower. Thus life is not devoid of such qualities, whose expression of beauty is nothing but the expression of love in the name of beauty that enchants the beauty of others. Such beauty of every living being begets an attraction that needs a distinct energy that is unseen or invisible, that is nothing but love. So, every life-like flower has kept on beautifying this vast tree of mankind. Therefore, you should cherish 'love' in your life. It will beautify and felicitate you. So, it is true that we all still suffer from lack of true beauty. As a result, the external beauty prevents us from knowing the true reality of our life.

It is beyond my knowledge whether I have enabled to express my intention to you why I have chosen this subject. If you think deeply, you may agree with me on this point. In this respect, I think that 'love' is only 'matter', only 'thing', only 'media' for beautifying and living and making everything peaceful in life. It can awaken 'humanity' in life. So the reality of love must be the first issue and the first lesson in life. I want you live a serene and a happy life taking 'love' to your heart.

FIRST CHAPTER

WHAT IS LOVE?

Some definitions are given to extend the uplifting range of the proper theme.

Ø Love is an unseen force, which keeps the wheel of the vast universe constant moving.

Ø Love is the greatest inspiration to inspire the living being to sustain the world productive.

Ø Love is the primal plough to plough this corporal body and mind (i.e. land of eight phenomena).

Ø Love is sex that sustains this beautiful creation alive, while sex is concomitant with the truth.

Ø Love is the first or the oldest friend to peep into the obscurity of man's mind.

Ø Love is a great pretext to shirk beastlike sex of man's body.

Ø Love is a true invisible matter, and this corporal body is its shadow.

Ø Love is a heavenly touchstone of which little contact makes a human body love laden object.

Ø Love is an unseen food of the unseen mind to provide real energy to fight against the untrue.

Ø Love is greatest relation and every being is its fragmentary relation.

Ø Love is a keen consciousness to sharpen the haunted consciousness of human mind.

Ø Love is a prime clue to finding out the obscure meaning of this singular life.

Ø Love is spirited to the spiritual heart.

Ø Love is light, but human body is its shadow.

Ø Love is spontaneous influx concerning life

Ø Love is a 'Beautiful hut'; it saves its occupants from any ruin and destruction.

Ø Love is the primal source of all creations in this universe.

Ø Love is the best supporter of life.

Ø Love is essence, so life is present.

Ø Love is inspiration, so life longs for expectation of a peaceful and happy life.

Ø Love is the best nurse to nurse man's worldly vanity of body.

Ø Love is extant, so life is spirited.

Ø Love is passion and emotion in every being to alleviate worldly anxiety and frustration.

Ø Love is an unasked guest to haunt your loving hut.

Ø Love is a breath; life is a sigh of breath.

Ø Love is philosophy and then life is peeping into its addicted body from behind philosophy.

Ø Love is an expression of beauty and sanctity amid this cursed life to purify this curse.

Ø Love is a main source of power that coincides with one another of eight elements, which consist of this body (i.e. mind, intelligence, pride, soil, water, fire, air and sky).

Ø Sublimity is the life of love, but subtlety is its Philosophy, while both coincided with each other in a human life, since then this being becomes a true lover or beloved.

Ø Love is such an invisible power of which presence makes you self-confident and self-reliant, but its absence makes you desolate and hopeless for going ahead of facing any obstacle.

Ø Love is a co-existence of mind and soul in the corporal body.

Ø Love is a source of all goodness expressed through human activities.

Ø Love makes the life from' good' to 'better' and 'better' to 'best'.

Ø Love is the best catalyst in the reaction of life regarding both body and mind.

Ø Love is a source of inspiration of any new invention of any man in this world.

Ø Love is the vitality of this gross-body.

Ø Love is the expression of the vitality of the spirited and life-like soul through sacred activities.

Ø Love is the great protest against blind belief, which leads a life to the destruction.

Ø Love is a bridge for crossing the ocean of life and the world.

Ø Love is a great vanity that gives birth to humanity.

Ø Love begets the fragmentary interest in life to enliven every moment as to this cursed life.

Ø Love is an introduction and conclusion in accordance to this mortal life.

Ø   Love is alteration between this life and the world.

Ø   this mortal frame is repulsion regarding real love; but love turns it into altercation for the essence of this frame.

Ø   Love is a dream to a man for want of humanity, but 'truth' to humanity.

Ø   Love is the sun and the life is the moon.

Ø   Love is the supreme source of expression of this life.

Ø   If this life is science, love will be philosophy.

Ø   Love is the truest knowledge to know this phenomenal life.

Ø   Love seems blind in the world but visible in mystery of life.

Ø   Love is an expression of the true fulfillment through this life.

Ø   Love begets true philosophy through this mortal life.

Ø   Love places co-existence between life and the world.

Ø   Love equalizes the balance between life and the world.

Ø   Love equalizes the balance between knowledge and science.

Ø Love is the most wonderful gift by God to this wonderful life in this world.

Ø Love is the greatest and the truest tune of this vast universe and life is its discordant and a broken tune.

Ø Love is the true perception amid conception of life.

Ø Love is true cause of all pleasures in this world.

Ø Love engrosses all animate being with its beautification, so every being looks beautiful.

Ø Love is the best measuring stick to measure the melting point of the solution of life and philosophy.

Ø Love is regarded as a prime media of measurement to find out nuance from man to man.

Ø Love is a purified name of an unseen attraction, which has combined five separate elements (i.e. earth, fire, water, space, air) together including other three invisible elements, namely mind, intelligence and pride into a human life.

Ø Love is the proper 'co-ordinates' of any place of the graph of this human life in respect of a true knowledge of a specific mind of the various persons.

Ø Love is the best rudder of this life-like 'ship' in the obscurity of this worldly ocean.

Ø Love acts like a doorkeeper to open the door of consciousness of a human life.

Ø Love is a reflection of attractive force of life, otherwise life would be motionless.

Ø Love is the balance among three inner stages of this human life, namely Gross body, reasoning body and subtle body.

Ø Love is the best ladder to reach the lofty position of this worldly life, on the basis of the Supreme worth of human quality.

Ø Love is the primal source of all fragmentary times, which keeps every life tuned in this world.

Ø Love is the force of subtle-feeling, which combines thousand of feelings together to get a conspicuous idea of ten organs and mind.

Ø Love begets the true hope and dream, and love leads them to a proper way.

Ø Love is the self-originated attractive energy of constituent elements out of which five visible and three invisible elements; which activate eleven organs of human life and guide them to go in their proper respective way.

Ø Love is a subtle central point of energy or force in a life in respect of various minds; that provides influx of energy to confront with any new matter.

Ø   A human life has three stages on the basis of knowledge; namely, gross-body, reasoning body and subtle body; these three stages are perceived in the same body of a human life. But knowledge seems latent in the first stage (i.e. gross body); so at this stage man is averse to love; but at the second stage (i.e. Reasoning body) man takes 'love' through reasoning; where knowledge is purified amid different reasoning activities; thus at this stage knowledge is enhanced or flourished under the influence of 'reasoning power' since then love engrosses man's different organs of perception and action; and in the midst of understanding on the basis of proper reason man accepts love as a reason or cause of his enjoyment and pleasure. But at the third stage, knowledge becomes sharp and transparent; so such a sharp knowledge makes a man hungry for realizing sharp and subtle knowledge, where love seems so conspicuous, though a man seems a worldly being, he is able to grasp and discern the subtle attraction of love with one another in this universe by dint of his sublime knowledge.

So, 'knowledge' is the best thing to elevate the essential organs of perception to the level of realization of love.

Ø   Man is a slave to love; because man is under its guidance or leadership.

Ø   Love is the teleology in the explanation of both the life and the world.

Ø Love is the main 'saviour' to save this mortal body from the blind belief of wreckage.

Ø Love is 'Brahma' which is the prime existence of this creation, because 'sound' is called 'Brahma' accordingly Indian philosophy; since this sound is nothing but 'energy' (i.e called sound energy). Besides, 'sound' comes into effect by vibration, so vibration begets sound amid a distinct media; but this vibration seems non—existing without unseen energy of attraction. If it is felt deeply, it will be clear that whenever any 'sound' produced by vibration through a man (i.e 'man' has been taken as an excellent example, because a man is vested with consciousness and knowledge); since then this 'sound' is not of love; because the unseen vibrate energy, which begets 'sound' on the basis of compact attractive energy displayed through vibration. The purified name of sound is 'tune', which is produced by a man having percolated amid knowledge and secret heart, then it can charm and attract the various organs of human body, and thus such attraction gives birth to love; and love also begets such attraction. Since then love is 'attraction', and 'attraction' is love. It is true in respect of media.

Ø A sound is produced by the combination of thousand of vibrations. These vibrations need attractive force or energy, because without this attractive force or energy 'vibration' will be valueless. So it is clear that attractive force begets vibration and this vibration begets also 'sound' whenever this sound becomes charming and sweet mixing with knowledge and consciousness derived from heart or mind of the man; then this sweet 'sound' turned into 'tune' to beget love in the mind of a man. Based on this discussion, hope it has been obvious to you. Hence 'Brahma' is 'love', and 'Brahma' never becomes a complete conception out of love. So, in every turn of life one must realize and feel that whatever occurs in this world is not possible without attractive force or energy. And its purified name, especially in a human life, is glorious.

Ø Man is always in quest of love to get its favour, not love is in the wake of man; though it seems outwardly.

Ø Love only can inspire a man with a proper hope and aim.

Ø Love is the greatest, the largest and the truest ocean of the emotion, where every life seems a little motion of the wave of this vast emotion.

Ø Love is the high way of the life where knowledge is the truest and the oldest friend of it. Consciousness is the oldest and an unasked guest to love; introspection is its philosophy, and the world is the glade of pleasure.

Ø Eternity is the last termination of love, when reality is an inception, and life is the media of realization concerning both reality and eternity.

Ø Love is constant; it takes different appearances through the different five organs as the media.

Ø Love gets life while organs of perception agreeing with one another based on mind; intelligence and pride, where knowledge will be man's great supporter.

Ø Love is god, when life becomes lively, spirited and speedy coming in contact with beauty, knowledge and consciousness.

Ø Love is caught in the grip of sight while the 'mind' sends its invitation in the midst of the eyes to feast of life.

Ø Love is a brilliant and beautiful 'look' of the 'beloved' and 'lover' while this look is substitute for the introspection that keeps into the very depth of the essence.

Ø Love may come of any beauty of human body, even any living being; (both man and woman); if this beauty maintains the equality and balance between reality and eternity.

Ø Human life is nothing but an expression of the vast attractive force; not only in human life but also in every living being. But this attractive force manifests itself in various ways through living beings. Here this attractive force and energy have expressed itself in the midst of human life in the name of love. Where knowledge plays the best role to guide and apply this love in every life.

Ø Love is an eternal hunger of a human life; because knowledge is eternal and immortal; so knowledge makes mind hungry for love. Since then love becomes eternal food of mind.

Ø Love is the beauty of the heart that appeases the agonized mind; not beauty of the outward of the corporeal body, which dazzles the eyes.

Ø Love is an incarnation of life.

Ø Love is the first and the last termination of this life like vehicle.

Ø Love is not a dreamy land; it is a land of reality to make a man realize (living being) about the hidden knowledge of life, the world and philosophy.

Ø Love is the first relation to acquaint this life with this universe.

Ø Love is the greatest ocean, and life is its main Island.

Ø Love is the totality and life is its fraction.

Ø Love is the vitality of the reality of this vast universe to realize the very essence of this vastness.

Ø Love is the first and last entrance regarding life and the World.

Ø Love is the best painkiller to assuage the agonized mind.

Ø Love is a purified power that results from the combination of invisible elements (earth, fire, soil, space and air) and three invisible elements (mind, intelligence and pride) that have expressed amid human body

Ø Love is the central point where life, world and philosophy have coincided with one another.

Ø Love is the best supporter to keep the balance of life in course of its riding on relating to this World.

Ø Love is the main demarcation between the light and the dark with respect to the Inner World of this life.

Ø Love begets a beautiful belief that is an incarnation of the hidden power, which is not out of love.

Ø Love is the most mysterious thing and all mysteries are subject to balance betwixt reality and eternity.

Ø Love is the source of all energies which convey energy to the perceptive organs and the internal organ mind, through the media of knowledge.

Ø Love is the greatest pride that guides this mundane life to the right path.

Ø Love is the main "index" of the labyrinth to lead life to its proper destination.

Ø Love is the majestic and magnanimous, where knowledge is the media for judging and feeling its true aspect through this life as a proper media.

Ø Love is the best tonic, as a sip of this tonic provides lots of energy to forget the exhaustion, tiredness and frustration of life for a prolonged period, but simple and earthly tonic's longevity is very short span, so are is called the best energy tonic.

Ø Love is an eternal vitality of life to struggle for finding out the reality of essence of life.

Ø Love is a subtle belief which keeps a balance of parity between the body and the mind regarding this universe.

Ø Love is a real science (i.e. special knowledge) of philosophy relating to life to discern and realize the coexistence of the present, the past and the future.

Ø Life does not know how it is conspicuous in the midst of LOVE.

Ø Here vanity is dominant, there life is bereft of true beauty of love, but the dominance of knowledge gives birth to a certain beauty of life.

Ø Love is the first latent inherent education of life that becomes flourished amid the explosion of the essence of individuality under the impact of both direct & indirect knowledge.

Ø   Love is the sweet nectar derived from the churning of the ocean of life, where vanity is poison.

Ø   Love is the simplification by dint of which magic touch life is freed from an arrant complication.

Ø   Life is a sort of installment' on the given love like loan manipulated by GOD himself.

Ø   Love is the key to unlock the door of pleasure.

Ø   Love is like the sharpest weapon to confront any lurking foe in the prolonged journey of life regarding the inner world.

Ø   Life seems to be a grandeur occasion where love the primal source of inspiration to carry it out.

Ø   Love is a vital force that enforces life ahead facing all types of hindrances in course of its prolonged journey to realize properly.

Ø   A true life is a complete circle in respect of any relation, where love is the central point to which life is constantly inclined to make a specific relation.

Ø   Love is like a centripetal force, which attracts all lives to its centre to centralize every life to its primal source.

Ø   Love is the centre of a triangle consisting of life, world and philosophy.

Ø Science is a special knowledge of any specific thing, like it love is also a special knowledge for realization of life. Hence love seems to be the greatest science regarding life without which the trickle of consciousness is nonexistent. So, the more you realize love, the more you will grasp the mystery of life.

Ø Life is relative in respect of love.

Ø Love is the golden ladder of heaven.

Ø Love is the first expression of the true existence. Hence life is an apparent expression of its hidden power.

Ø Love is a constant motion, so life seems speedy.

Ø Love is sweet, sweeter and the sweetest pursuant to imbue knowledge of a man.

Ø Love is a heavenly shower to awaken the latent feeling to feel the true essence of life.

Ø Love is disparity to vanity, but equability to beauty.

Ø Love is the supreme guest to the hut of life.

Ø Love seems to be a 'unit' to any solved problem relating to life; where life is just like a distinct 'problem' whose ultimate result' will be valueless without love.

Ø Love is a full-fledged expression of consciousness.

Ø Love is an acute flavour of life that hovers and fills the air, and sweetens the pungent atmosphere of the insipid life.

Ø Love is valourity to surmount the odyssey of life.

Ø Love is that thing which makes a man think of the liberation of life from this Worldly bondage.

Ø Love is an unknown miracle stick gifted by creator to alleviate pain and sorrow by touching of it.

Ø Love is the first and foremost entity to verify man's real identity.

Ø Love is not only dream but also a ray of heaven, which makes a life always even, not uneven.

Ø Love is the first sight in the midst of which the vast universe becomes visible.

Ø Love is the best quality for the animate and inanimate, human, for 'humanity' and 'coolness' for water.

Ø Love is not only a dreamy world but also the reality of dream coinciding with eternity of dream.

Ø Love is an unseen speedy vehicle which makes a man run from one place to another to realize the unknown.

Ø Love is the completeness in the incompleteness concerning this life.

Ø In the absence of love, sex brings only incompleteness regarding true pleasure of Life.

Ø whatever we see is apparently real, but love occurs true realization.

Ø Love is a sweet tremor of voice which enchants both life and the world with its spell of the subtlety.

Ø Love is the true mirror for observing the real feature of life.

SECOND CHAPTER

LOVE ITSELF BEGETS ITS OWN MEANING

How sweet and wonderful this creation is!

How majestic and grandeur this occasion is!

The known and the unknown gather here

By attraction of the inner hidden true power;

They seem utterly strange with one another,

Yet they look so friendly like and cheer.

The most people are still unaware of its mystery. Why? Let us advance to the expected point of discussion to divulge the shroud of love concerning this vast creation I wish to make this matter conspicuous also through the graph. In this chapter I endeavour to bring the core theme of this book.

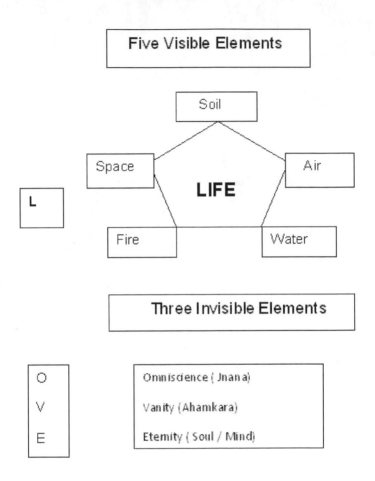

The mélange of each hidden specific power of eight elements resulted in a distinct sublime power in human body. This human body is non-existent without these eight elements. This sublime power is realized and grasped by the pure knowledge that is only dominant in human life owing to the presence of three invisible elements. It is called purified power. Love is the lofty and the dignified name of this purified power. Man is the best of all creations, because 'man' is the true expression of this Purified Power, so man is above all and also superior to others. If you are asked to ponder over this matter, are you beyond it? On this point, love is the source of all creations. It exists in all as an innermost invisible power and provides necessary power to keep all speedy. I hope the above discussion will solve your immanent and puzzling questions. So, where is life, there is love. Without existence of love, life can't be realized. And in absence of love life remains locked. It never discloses its mystery, entity and magnanimity. Hence life tastes bitter throughout its prolonged span. If you cherish this purified power (love) in your life, you'll not be floated in the ocean of sorrow. I request all of you to cogitate over it to carry your burdened life smoothly and spontaneously to its destination.

THIRD CHAPTER

PLACE 'I' ON 'LOVE', NOT 'LOVE' ON 'I'

Without love 'I' is vanity

That is void of true beauty:

'I' is a fragmentary of love

Which keeps 'I' above?

Under the compulsion of an exquisite proclivity I have held my pen to write this chapter. I am not a poet, so I have no capacity to imbue your mind with imagination and dream. I am neither the author nor a writer, nor a novelist—I am devoid of all good qualities. I am now sitting before an open window. It is at about 2 a.m. Only, at this moment, the darkness is enveloping in about me with its most silent footstep. Even I am not able to see anything in a distance but the silent laughter of dense-dark. Yet a few fireflies are scattering light that seems to be the distant stars. At times some stars are peeping from the behind dark cloudy sky. Perhaps, the span of this darkness will last for a few hours.

Though the darkness of the night is for a few hours, yet we manage several necessary media for getting light and driving the darkness such as lantern, lamp, electricity etc. But, have we thought of the darkness, which we have been still carrying on in our mind? That is thicker than the darkness of night; even it is the darkest of all. Now, if you are asked—who likes living in the darkness? And who lives in the darkness? Is it possible for you to live a peaceful life in the darkness? So, to make our life comfortable and sweet we need 'light' at night, because we are human beings. We are still ahead of other beings in this world in respect of civilization, tradition, consciousness, knowledge and intelligence, for we are called the best creation. We are not accustomed to the external darkness so we need 'light'. In this respect we are surely the inhabitants of the world of light. Being an inhabitant of the world of light, why are we getting lost ourselves in the darkness day after day? Hence a beast can't be differentiated from a 'best'. Are we not inferior to a beast? Though the creator has imparted all to us, in spite of having we all are blind yet. So, a question may arise, what is the difference between a 'best' and a 'beast'? Is it not true? Men are merely the best creation in a manner of thinking externally. If we ponder over ourselves, it will be transparent that we are still in the deepest darkness of ignorance. Despite remaining all necessary elements for driving this darkness away, we have forgotten to apply these in the right time. So we are groping and lamenting for light! If anybody asks— who are you? I mean, I am 'I', and here the meaning of 'I' is vanity, egoism, and pride. So, if you are asked and requested to think of 'I'; what will you think of it? This 'I' is loaded with vanity, pride, egoism and selfishness—and these seem to be the obstacles to come over this illusive 'I'. 'I' means a part of great relation, like 'I', 'you', 'he', and 'she', Ram, Shyam etc. give specific relations concerning different acquaintances.

Before I have spoken of this aspect; yet I put a little emphasis on it. 'I' or 'you' and etc. are nothing but a beam of light reflected from love like sun. But we have lost our that vision to glimpse out the essence of 'I', which supports this 'I', on which 'I' is still standing, otherwise it would be valueless and meaningless. Even this vastness also would be void of beauty', because this vast universe consists of 'I'. As 'I' begets beauty, beauty also begets 'I',—here 'beauty' is a splendid reflection of love through 'I'. it is sure whenever 'beauty' means a ray of love is reflected through 'I', since then this 'I' is no more vested with vanity and egoism. It becomes then a pride of a great truth. So all persons seem to be individual of 'I', and love is the life of this 'I'. Can you think of anything relating to life without love? On this point of discussion, I request all of my readers and friends to enhance 'yourself (i.e. 'I') on the basis of love, so you will feel a remarkable thrill of pleasure and joy which must help you to tide over meanness, egoism, inhumanity, vanity and pride. These are beneath the dignity of humanity' and your individuality and personality will be sweet and delighted. As a result, both your personal and family life will be beautiful and happy. Do you not seek after such a happy and a peaceful life being a man?

Love exists everywhere. So, it is called omnipresence. Even it exists in the tinniest particle of dust and the smallest drop of water. If not, this ocean and mountain would be non-existing. Love means a kind of alteration existing both in the inanimate world and the animate world. It can be only felt with subtle feeling on the basis of Philosophy. but 'love' seems to be lively in the animate. So, man is the best of all the animate belonging to the world of the animate. For this reason, 'love' longs for the animation, and the life through man. So, without love life is a lifeless thing. It is obvious that loveless life is just like a beast of the darkness. So, I request you to love and manifest yourself through love having placed 'you' or 'I' on the altar of love. You try your best to establish yourself of your 'I' on the basis of love. You never place 'Love' on 'you' or 'I', because 'I' is weaker than love. 'Love' can never be placed on 'I'. 'Love' begets 'I'. Love expresses itself through 'I'. So under the influence of 'love' 'I' seems to be loveable and beautiful. 'I' is just like the moon that has not its own light. It is lighted by of the sun. So it looks beautiful. We take the moon, as a symbol of beautification mistakenly, if the light of the sun is taken off the man gets lost in the darkness. So, man takes the moon as a symbol of the beauty mistakenly, because the sun makes the moon beautiful and shining. Just like 'I' looks beautiful, sweet, and sincere with view to attracting for true love. When this 'I' comes in contact with another 'I', it turns into beauty. And true 'I' which longs for partaking of sweet nectar' and is freed from all anxieties. But, without love 'I' is egoistic and ugly, though externally it seems to be splendid and beautiful. So this beauty and pleasure of 'I' don't last forever, this seems to be ephemeral glory. Perchance, you have understood what I have desired to tell you. Though

we are educated, intelligent and clever, we have lost
our realizing power for the grasping of the essence of
essential qualities and characteristics that are vested with
our individual life. So we are overwhelmed with the
redundant beauty of love that brings about a sorrowful
sequel in our life. As a result, we are becoming readily
the victims of the frustration that has made our personal
and family life rancorous.

This modern world seems to be immersed in the
billowy ocean of love. Yet it can't wipe out the rueful
tear of bitterness from the eyes of man, because
one tries to establish one's life through love without
testing one's 'I' with the help of touchstone of love.
So, it seems insecure. One is again requested to
judge 'oneself' (i.e. 'I') by touchstone of love, so all
characteristics of 'I' namely vanity and selfishness
etc. will be vanished. Then one must come in contact
with proper love and its magic touch must give one a
world of joy and vanishes all sufferings, anxieties and
frustrations from life. Remembering that, this love
brings fame, honour, wealth and heavenly happiness
in the individual and family life also. My readers!
Are you not desirous of sustaining such a happy and
pleasant life having shaken off this spurious masking
of love from your life? You look around; you must see
that 'love' is still waiting at Royal gate of life like an
unasked or an uninvited guest with tearful eyes. Let
'Love' haunt your hut'. Don't drive 'her' away; don't
frown at 'her'. Don't show aversion to her; take 'her' in
your heart! I fear whether I kill your precious time or
not. If not, I send a handful of love through this poor
expression of my destitute heart

Respecting a distinct outlook, this vast Nature even exists because of the sun. In the presence of the sunlight the green live on through different scientific systems and reactions. Both the sun and the soil provide silently Nature with food, so Nature looks lively and fresh and beautiful. Such function in this nature is going on in an invisible manner. And love also provides you invisible food. this nourishes your unseen mind, and your mind is spontaneously partaking of this pabulum and is getting healthy gradually and effortlessly. As this food (i.e. love) is not seen with the naked eyes, and the mind, which accepts this food, not be visible. So it never leaves any trace behind externally. When it's true influence will fall upon you, only you will be able to realize, how you are in a good humour and in a sincere mood with a peaceful mental satisfaction. One should keep in mind that such food (i.e. love) is an antidote against all fatal and chronic maladies, which prevent one from having a happy and peaceful life both in respect of personal and family life. So, it is evident that love is the best supporter of you. (i.e. when yourself express 'you', 'you' then is turned into 'I'). And here 'I' is the best explanation of all. Without love 'I' is valueless and meaningless. If you long for a happy life, you must fully depend on love. Love is an unseen food to your unseen mind. Both are invisible, so both are true. The world of 'I' means the world of human being individually. The essence of 'I' exists in love' and love provides 'I' with existence. On considering the discussion, it will be pellucid to you that you are nothing but a shadow of love. So you are in the wake of love, it means you (i.e. 'I') are a concomitant with love.

The more you partake of love, the more you have fortitude in your mind to confront any frustration and sorrow in life to hug the happy shore of the life-ocean. Dear friend! By grace of which you are extant. You are related to the others with different relations. But you are really blind of realizing. You are ignorant of discerning that real friend who has been keeping you smiling and life-like always. If you are averse to knowing and even averse to sacrificing for your well wisher (i.e. love) how do you expect a happy life? To have a blithe life you should not fritter a minute for a while! Don't kill your venerated moment thinking away in an awkward way. You forget the past to sweeten the present. Your first act is to love intently. And your second duty is to make your love fruitful in your every inch of life. And your third duty is to procure a friendly relation among your relatives and close ones amid love in a true way. Later you will find that your personal world will be greater and wide, though you are a poor fellow in the matter of worldly wealth. However, love is likely a persistent, unasked and untimely friend-cum-guest at your door, but you are too shameless to treat her to any gorgeous feast in your life.

FOURTH CHAPTER

IS SEX NOT LOVE?
IF IT IS, WHY & WHEN?

Sex is a great pretext to slake this body:

In absence of love turned into muddy

I do mind this is a vital chapter to make the theme of the book more ostentatious concerning 'love' and 'sex' without which life is meaningless. So, an exquisite idea has impelled me to write this chapter that will tell what I have intended to explicate here. How would this beautiful creation be possible without sex and love? Sex is a great pretext to sustain this vast and splendid creation amid love being concomitant with sanctity and truth. Sex is a profound attraction under the influence of love. But always you have to keep in mind that sex must be love, and love must be sex, whenever this sex must be synchronous with sanctity and truth. If not, this creation would never be possible. If creation were not extant, love would be non-existent in this world. If it is pondered deeply over this beautiful creation, it will be evident that this creation exists in presence of attraction. Here such attraction is nothing but an unseen force or power, which keeps closely both the animate and the inanimate things with one another. And such attraction has come of love. Love is a strong attraction, because love is a purified name of the attractive force, which attracts all to its center in the most exquisite way. So, another name of the attraction is 'creation'. And this unseen force of attraction keeps the vastness speedy. Truly speaking, such attraction is nothing but 'love'. The whole creation is overwhelmed with this attraction. In this world nothing is occurred frequently without such attraction. So long as, this attraction is present, this creation also exists. We never think of beautiful any creation without a hopeful attraction. Now I want to tell about 'love'. Concerning this, a question may arise in accordance with 'creation',—namely, 'man is the best and the sweetest creation in this world. How does this sweetest creation come into effect accompanied by love? It is very much mysterious and the occult. In the next chapter I desire to throw my poor outlook upon this matter.

Please, let me delineate now regarding 'sex'—when it is concomitant and not concomitant with love. Now my discussion is that a creation means 'man' who comes in to this world through the sexual attachment of two hearts (i.e. a male and female). It is not out of our thought. Since birth love is infused into this sweetest creation called "man", though no being is out of it (i.e. "man" has been taken as an example, because it will be better in respect of discussing regarding love).So, every man (i.e. life) is vested with love. Which love is creative or destructive? Here is a question:—is love ever being destructive? If not, why is it possible? I intend to expose it to you. My friends wait a little before I have already told you that love is sex, and sex is love while accompanying with sanctity and beauty. I hope you should have had a back up of your question from this, because whenever a life (i.e. man) comes into being through the sexual relation of two hearts, male and female on the basis of the truth. It means here sex goes with the truth. Hence life is associated with purified soul, and this mortal body or gross body is still purified with the possession of pure love. Such life obsessed with love begets a sacred soul crowned with love. Such creation seems to be creative, because such life has come into this world through sex being associated with love. And it is called love like sex. Since "love" is sex. And such life tries best to rectify the life, which is born through blind sex and passion on the basis of the gross attraction only.

In spite of remaining love in life (i.e. man) men are hostile to one another. If not, this world must be turned into heaven. Here would not be any jealousy, vanity and pride from man to man and from heart to heart So long, perhaps, you have discerned this vital discussion. I welcome you to enjoy this expectant life as to both personal and family aspects through sex, passion and emotion. But you ought to be conscious of "love" which must be concomitant with sanctity. So you must have a profound peace and elation. And love must stay with you as an oldest friend to prevent you from associating with any frustration and anxiety.

If you expect to have such a blissful life, I request you not to single "love" and drive it away from your door.

You greet "love" to your destitute heart. Don't forget her in your distress, because "love" is an usher of a prolonged happiness. Don't dawdle away time in vain, please you keep your sweet-heart in your yearnful heart and cast your two expected looks into her two beatific looks and try your best to find out the essence of her sight. You will find that there is love and love while casting your fervent glimpse around. Now a puzzling question is: why does the life look hopeless and gloomy? Here this life should have become fresh, lively and hopeful, but day-by-day life gets complicated and involved in a non-stop problem. Where life would have become easy, smooth as well as pleasant, there it has become complex. It means that such love makes a life intricate, and it is nothing but destructive. But proper love rests on creativity. If you ask yourself, it will be clear that gradually we are involving into a gross sex. Men are so anxious for satisfying their physical hunger, which is void of sanctity and beauty. Though it seems to be love outwardly, it is not a true love. It is so-called a deceptive and an emotional attraction which seems to be gorgeous and splendid externally. Such love is nothing but bodily attraction for sexual satisfaction. That love never lasts for a long period can't be a true love. Such love in life comes into being on the basis of outside physical beauty. It is obvious that almost our modern love is loaded with gross sex only without being concomitant with the truth because modernity is too sophisticated to praise simplicity. So its sequel is destructive, and life becomes more problematic. Despite love around you there is only outburst of frustration and hopelessness, because it is a mere passion called sophisticated love, not a fair love.

So, our life is just like a depressed football because a football is a football whether it is depressed or not. But, when it is filled with wind, it gets its full shape and will be suitable then for fulfilling the objective of people, because 'wind' is the essence of this football. As 'wind' not be seen, be felt only by sharp knowledge. Like a depressed ball, our life is also depressed for want of its essence called "love". From the outside every man is called a man, though he is depressed like a football for want of unseen essence called love internally. Since love is also unseen. No mortal limb can touch practically. Only subtle feeling and consciousness can feel it. When man is void of love, he is nothing but a depressed football. Then he is merely a man who is not considered as a good one for others. So, his life seems non-existent as man. Such man is like a depressed football regarded as an obstruction. Therefore without love, a life becomes a mere gross-life. Then it becomes a non-appreciated matter everywhere. In accordance with the above discussion, I again welcome and invite you to embrace a happy life and get a world of joy through love being rested on sanctity and simplicity. And it is clear that sex is a great pretext to relish the felicity of this gross body in absence of love. Such felicity is harmful and detrimental to both your personal and family life. It has no any good objective. So, that life is associated with such a gross-felicity is nothing but a nightmare. And love seems an enigma then. Without knowing the real essence of love, men are busy to make their life comfortable and happy on delusive love, so men under go many impediments. In order to prolong one's pleasure and sweeten one's cursed life and beautify one's life one should try to place one's gross life on sanctity and beauty rousing one's latent faculties in the question of humanity. Since then one feels and realizes the true love that must be one's alter ego. And true love never leaves anyone in the lurch. Having come in contact with such love, one's gross life will turn into reasoning life, and into subtle life. Do you not yearn for such blessed love? Do you not desire to bring a lasting smile on your beloved face? Do you not enlarge your span of pleasure in your life? Why are you sitting and thinking away? Please, try your best to turn your every gross moment into a lasting moment through love. Then you will be a successful man being propelled all grief from your gross life. And you'll be able to place your goddess of love on the altar of your heart. Love becomes lovely while cherishing lovingly in the life with help of five sense organs and an internal organ (i.e. organs of perception namely eye, ear, nose, tongue and skin, and mind).

FIFTH CHAPTER

HAVE YOU HAD YOUR LOVE?

O' Love! O' my beloved

Come and hold my hand,

O' Spirit! You are above all,

Without you Life is gall

For whom you have spent many an hour, many a day, many a month and many a year of your life. For whom you have left a long road behind you to get her warm contact of love. For whom you once became a mad. Even you did not hesitate to go against all members of your family that was your first place of your childhood for the game of hide and seek. Besides, you had to leave your all relatives to build up a dreamy-hut of love with your lover. At last you did that. You have entered the family making him or her prince or princess in your life. For whom you had shed much tear and sweat—what have you had at last?

Where you should have expected to get an immense pleasure and longed for a peaceful and happy life, there you have had nothing but a handful of frustration. Irony of fate is against you. Now your life is swinging like a dried leaf. Perhaps, it may drip instantly under the impact of a stormy wind. Your every moment is overcast with the cloud of despair. You are going to relinquish the hope of your life. Why?

Above ninety percent people are facing this difficult to overcome. Their appearance is just like a victim of famine. Day after day they are getting immersed into despondency. Where is that colourful day? Where is your love-letter wrapped with colourful envelope? Where is your those sweet moonlit nights while gossiping and whispering lying your hand on her or on his hands, and keeping your thirsty looks into her or into his looks, and drinking and sucking sweet nectar of your lover or beloved throughout night? If you are asked now: Are you happy? Have you had your true love? Have you obsessed by an illusion of love? Have you ever portrayed the sweet feature of love on your mind? Have you had true love from your lover or beloved? Despite two eyes you are really blind. You have lost your taste in spite of your tongues. you have also killed your perception and introspection in presence of your mind. of course, you are a forlorn. Having been brought up in the lap of love you are really ignorant of it like a conch and an oyster. Though they came into being in the lap of ocean, yet they are fully unknown about this. It is a matter of shame because being a man you are still committing mistake blindly. for this sad plight nobody is responsible for you. you are responsible for yourself. Because, according to the law of Nature you have come in to this beautiful world with all necessaries. Yet you are too idle and lazy to long for knowing about yourself. Despite your power and energy you don't apply your knowledge to realize the true fact. My friend! Thus you don't destroy your sacred moment involved into the obsession of emotion. You try your best to be an endeavourer of true love, so you will be able to soothe your cursed life by touching its golden stick. In this respect I wish to say that every living being is a splendid media of love. But human life is the best and the most remarkable media for the manifestation of the true essence of love because human life is comprised of different vital and essential elements together where love has exposed itself spontaneously. If you go to the very bottom of the heart of both the animate and the inanimate thing, it is nothing but the hidden force of love. For this reason, human life is the best media of love, because love has spread its all charms in human life. As a result, the relish of love is the sweetest of all. So, one is so eager to have its taste at risk of one's life.

Regarding this, everybody should take a lesson on 'love', because it is the best learning in human life. But people have been ignoring such lesson as to love. So, every life, even the whole of the world is getting embroiled in the endless pugnacious ness and vanity. These are against the truth and humanity. In order to take this lesson on love, you should not need to go to any man made institution. Always everybody should think that his life is his best institution for getting lesson on love. True lesson about love is a proper knowledge of love. This lesson is a vital matter in man's life. Besides, it plays the key role to guide this life to a distinct destination. Whenever you will be able to get such lesson from your own life being a master of your own self, you will be astonished at and glad of procuring lesson about love by yourself. But one is more eager to get a beautiful flower of distant place than the flower that is still blooming in front of the window of one's reading room, though it is more beautiful than that flower.

On this point, it is obvious that we are not extant in our essence. We are always anxious for others in respect of ins and outs without rousing any curiosity about our self. So, it is a great mistake in our life. Having caught hold of whose hand you have come into this way of life, you don't hesitate to forget his or her gift. Really we are a great violator of the truth, though love is nothing but the true expression of the truth, and this truth is the best guide of us, in absence of which we are meaningless, yet we are blind. Though man is a wonderful being, he is not able to reach at the bottom of realizing of his own world. Being a remarkable creation man is benighted of such mystery. For this reason, he needs a lesson about 'love'. Those who have enabled to love lovingly having the true knowledge of their own essence, they find it possible to get at the brink of love. Since then they are really happy men. If a student does not prepare his lesson regularly and attentively he is punished and rebuked by his teachers and tutors, even by his parents. It means his studentship gets ignored and he feels a great shame among his classmates. If you are not able to learn your lesson of 'love' in a proper way you will be also punished and rebuked by your own consciousness like an inattentive student. because, for want of proper lesson respecting love you will not be able to manifest your duties in your personal and family life. it seems that every duty in your life gets disordered. So you feel frustration and uneasiness at every step in your life. Truly speaking, every act in every life has been put in an order like flowers, which are chained in a garland. so life is nothing but a garland made of orderly flowers of love. Whenever a single flower is displaced from the garland, the whole of the garland looks incongruous. a life is also like an inconsistent garland while deserting love (i.e. like a flower) from any corner of life, Man then falls instantly in despair. And he feels too enervated to advance ahead struggling.

Come closer to my pen and listen patiently to its whispering agony for a while. We have come into this beautiful large family with high hope to have much pleasure and rejoice in our life. Can you call up the first day when you had been initiated with a garland this garland was nothing but a garland of sacred blessing of Lord, made of love-flowers. Please, my friend, you try your best to keep the honour of this initiated garland. So you will be happy, and spirited at every step of life. Perhaps, I shall not be able to provide you with food and pelf and shelter but a few words. Perchance it may bring a ray of hope in your agonized life to give a hint of light removing the darkness of life. I have nothing but my writings, which are expression of my poor heart may impart you a sigh of relief to your exhausted life. Life is nothing but a desert without pleasure. And love is the main source of all pleasure. So, in order to get and give this pleasure to others you are always struggling; but you are not able to have your expected result in comparison with your struggle, why? Have you asked about this to your own essence? Why are you getting defeated again and again in life? Besides, as many times, you are trying your best to build up a sweet and dreamy hut of love so much but it comes into ashes.

Why does 'love' not respond to your call? Why does 'love' not yield to you? 'Love' never yields to man until man yields to love because man is but a shadow or expression of love's force. You should keep in mind that—whenever you will yield to 'love', love will expose itself to you. As a result love is the essence of life force. Since then you will be able to charm others with your 'love'. Even if you are not able to get initiated yourself into the mysterious of love with sprinkling love-like holy water; so, you have no access to the secret of love. In which state men are still living nothing but a trance of emotion, not a conspicuous idea of love.

So, to get a manifest idea of love one must sacrifice one's life for an ideal love. I have tried utmost to discuss this before you through graph. Please, try to grasp what I intend to tell you. We are a discordant tune to the harp of the vastness. our stream of thought in a zigzag course compared with the right path of this universe. our consciousness is nothing but an inspiration of great love, yet we are still blind in the state of emotion. And we are the inconsistent in respect of the universal consistency. So, if you are a ripple of the ocean of the vast population, I am a little bubble on the surface of this little wave, and if you are a deep 'thought' in this struggling life I am a sigh of relief in your deep thought.

SIXTH CHAPTER

PROPER MEDIA BEGETS PROPER LOVE

What is right or wrong?

Cannot be known,

That is only possible

By love touch-stone.

I think this chapter will be very much fruitful and indispensable in your life. If you think deeply, it will be conspicuous to you. For the want of proper media life can't transpire its proper love through different relations. Always remembering that everything needs a specific media without which nothing can disclose its camouflaged characteristics and qualities spontaneously. So, one should need a proper media to manifest one's characteristics in a full-fledged.

So I discuss this chapter to sketch a distinct inkling of it. In life its usefulness is very much necessary. Perhaps you may take it as a trivial matter. If you do it, you'll be wrong about your judgment. Listen to what I intend to expatiate upon this expected subject matter.

Every life is like a piece of sandalwood, because life is rather similar to it respecting the innermost meaning. So I prefer this example to make you appreciate easily the proper purport of the expected matter. I believe that you have enough knowledge of a piece of sandalwood. The more you rub it, the more it will emit fragrance. Even it gives out the fragrance till finishing. To get fragrance from a piece of sandalwood, you need a piece of flat stone. So a piece of flat stone is the proper media for a piece of sandalwood. Please, wait a little. Let me explain it clearly, my readers!

You are asked to take four pieces of wood in equal size. And it is taken that one of the four pieces is a piece of sandalwood. If you put these four pieces of wood on any place, you are asked to tell from a distance, which is the sandalwood? Is it possible by you to tell? You will answer, 'No', because it is very difficult task to find out the proper piece of wood without touching and application. But when you are asked to touch these pieces you will be able to tell properly, because the right application helps you to pick up the right one.

My subject matter is 'media'. Already I've touched upon it. Let me exhibit evidently. You know that a piece of sandalwood needs a piece of flat stone to emit its fragrance spontaneously. If you rub it (i.e. sandal wood) against anything such as Iron, wood and brick etc. you will get hardly fragrance in comparison with a piece of flat stone. Perhaps, you must have realized why I have wished to bring out this example. On this point, I hope you must grasp what I intend to tell. Like a piece of sandalwood, each life is a specific media. So, the media of a man will be a man. It is obvious that everyman is crowned with various qualities and characteristics. Because you know that the different persons vary in their assorted qualities and dispositions. In this case, your proper media will be such man whose characteristics and qualities will be alike to your inner proclivities. Since you will be able to realize those faculties approximately flourished through the invisible attractive force by man's inherent characteristics. It is he or she who will be your proper media.

Otherwise, it will be contrary to you, because the wrong media always misguides a man. As a result, throughout your life you will not be able to have proper happiness, until you are able to arouse your sleeping faculties of life. And the regret fullness of personal life pervades worried ness and sadness. So, one must be conscious of selecting especially one's life partner with whom one intends to start one's life journey amid incessant struggles.It is very difficult and hard task to seek out the proper media in life. Without sacred heart love is not possible in a beautiful way. It is a matter of thinking that love is always above all worldly grieves and worries. That love is loaded with frustration' is far different from the cruel (earthly) 'frustration', which weakens the strength of mind to go forward and think of reaching a lofty position of life.

So, the lack of proper media makes the life unbearable. And life is downed with heavy worldly burdens. To get the golden touch of love at first one needs proper heart for one's longing heart. So, in the case of selecting your life partner (i.e. wife, beloved, lover, and friend etc) seem to be a media. You must be conscious of this matter. So people are day after day sinking into the bottomless suffering and frustration both in their personal and family life owing to neglecting of selecting their proper media.

It is a matter of astonishment that being man we are destitute of human qualities. Until you are able to manifest your love in your personal life you find it very hard to place a real peace in the other life by yourself. Always you have to think that without you a family is not complete, because you are the main cause of producing a family. So, to adorn every chapter of your life sequentially your first duty will be to dispel the disparity and diversity from your personal life on the basis of love that plays a key role in the making of relation with one another.

I could not but pointing out another example in this respect to do make this matter transparent to my readers because this example seems to be easier. Yet its depth is much enough. Listen to what my pen intends to whisper to you. (Perhaps, if you are able to dive into the bottom of this discussion, I hope what mistake you are committing may come to a close instantly.) We live in the modern age. So we all try to keep pace with the taste of modernity. I can think you have T.V Set, Radio Set and other electronic Sets etc. at your home as the sources of recreation. Suppose, your Radio Set has been out of order. It needs repairing. And your Radio Set is of Philip Company's model. Now you have to go to a Radio maker. Going there you give your Radio Set to the maker for repairing. The maker examined the Radio Set and told you to change a part of it. Having heard it you ordered him to replace this part by a new one. Then the Radio maker replies that he has not the machinery part of the same company. What he has is the same part of another company. He tells that it will not produce an original sound, which you could have got by the part of Phillip Company's model. Hearing this you request him to replace the old part by new one of other company's model. Here is the point of thinking regarding the subject. Like that our life has been disparate everywhere. We can't fill up the proper gap with proper thing. So life is left with endless pores of emptiness and has also been incongruous everywhere. As a result, your life will be a leafless tree in winter. And life will look dull losing its greenness of love. Without love man's life becomes tarnish and crazy shaking its love-like leaves. So it is sure that we are a mere man in respect of humanity. We are just like a Sodom. After all, life is a victim of utter disparity.

You had better think a little of this matter. Thus, if you use the wrong 'thing' in lieu of proper thing life will be uneven in its long course. You know what will be in long run? Yet we are using indiscriminately the unexpected and unsuitable 'thing' in our every step of life. As a result, we ourselves are responsible for our own dolour. And disparity prevails all over life. Even every step in our personal life is engulfed by frequent disparity. So, nothing can be led precisely without proper media. Always you should think that wrong and unsuitable media give birth to a incongruity.

Besides it is a point of thinking that nothing can be guided properly by the influence of force. Everything in this beautiful world is guided by the universal aw of Nature. So you are not out of these rules. Truly speaking, on the basis of the panoramic outlook man can't create whatever is vested with life because a subtle and mysterious hidden power act behind it. And one who procures this hidden power beyond this visible creation is called by different names by different classes of people with their true belief and sincerity. I think you have enough knowledge of it. So I don't want to extend this matter. But, as the sun has kept living the outside world, like that love has kept the entire inner world living of human mind. In the absence of the light of love like sun you must get lost yourself in the world of darkness of inhumanity. Love is beyond touching and seeing; and mind is also beyond touching and seeing. Both are invisible. In wider sense, whatever seems to be invisible that is real true and sacred. To find out the mystery of life man sticks to struggle. However, mind is the proper media of love. So love expresses itself through mind and spreads its invisible power and energy in life and depends on the capacity of mind.

In spite of knowing we are still indiscriminately committing fatal mistakes, because we are accustomed to seeing and facing such blunder in our family and society. Before I have already discussed that we have no any wish to think of and dive into the bottom of inner world of essence. Only we are wearing the feigned mask to dazzle the eyes of others. Really we are ignorant of essence of our self. But man does not know how such mistake paves the way for the grave of the crucial frustration day after day.

SEVENTH CHAPTER

KISS IS BLISS OF HEAVEN

Love is the most wonderful gift by God

To this wonderful life in this world,

It ascends just like a heavenly kiss

And turned this life in to a bit of bliss

A kiss is an external sign or an expression or an impression of love, affection or a tending-desire of this corporeal body. And this corporeal body is a better media for expressing love amid several distinguished fragmentary media. In this respect, a kiss seems to be the first and foremost media to imply love towards others. If one can ponder intensely one must be conscious of its esoteric and subtle application. Having centered love, the stream of heavenly bliss comes down this mundane world amid human life. Considering relation, every kiss ushers the heavenly bliss in life. A wave of the ocean can wash all weeds and dirt away from the shore in a trice. Kisses like a wave of the ocean of love can awash your all sullenness, anxiety, sadness and mournfulness away and can refresh you like a new-bloomed flower. Always you have to keep in mind that a kiss is an implication of your consciousness. A life cannot flourish fully for want of kiss of love, as a sweet bud can't open its dreamy eyes without the kissing of the sweet light of the rising sun. So, that life is devoid of kiss of love is bereft of the bliss of heaven. Even this beautiful creation would never be possible without the auspicious bliss of God, but this bliss descended to this earth to beautify and felicitate it through lots of kiss of love. so, love has begotten this penchant creation. At the dawn of your life, you first opened your eyes with your mother's sweet kiss. The invisible force of a mother's kiss grows you up and awakens gradually your dormant faculties in this hopeless world.

I wish you not to forget to have the heavenly bliss amid the kisses of love in your life. I don't know whether I disturb you or not. Yet I shall request you once for all to cogitate this matter. Please, you ask yourself. Are you not devoid of this bliss? Has your life teemed with heavenly bliss? Please my friend; don't cast your head down with shame or sad! Truly speaking, we all have forgotten to have bliss and give bliss because we are beyond the reach of kiss of love. Our consciousness is too blunt to catch the sharp glimpse of subtle pleasure of kiss, which is ushering the bliss in our life. Love is a great ocean; life is a small island of love. Then kiss is a flash of billowy wave on it. If life is an incarnation of love, your true knowledge must be a 'kiss' of which romantic contact will bring bliss in your cursed life. As a kiss is a sign of an extreme desire, bliss is a sign of pleasure. So both are substitute for each other, if a life seems to be a container of the sweet-nectar, We are still suffering from the penury of consciousness. So life has become dull and monotonous. Day-after-day life is getting tired of losing its vigour, liveliness. A brave heart or a mind is suitable for partaking of heavenly bliss through kiss being synchronous with knowledge. Those who are physically brave are not really courageous ones regarding true knowledge. Only sacred heart can triumph over the world of love. If a kiss comes of love, it will be able to provide life with vigour, vitality and energy to confront any hindrance in the way of your peace. Such a kiss is more energetic and strong. That kiss results from love becomes a source of an immense pleasure. If you are requested to think of yourself in the light of consciousness and to go back to the lost tracks of your life apropos of love, perhaps you may get a trace of love in your life, even you may have a taste of the kiss of your mother, that was the first bondage of sign of love had been impressed on you. So, we are all confined to this bondage. In course of life you can still confine yourself to this tie of kiss relating to different relations. If you realize this matter, you must grasp that nobody is out of this bondage of kiss. I want all of you to take this tie of 'kiss' directly or indirectly in your life. Always keep in mind that love is a gift of God. Whatever seems to be resulted from love is God's bliss. And this human life is the best media of love through which heavenly bliss always peeps into (here god seems to be an incarnation of most sublime power that is beyond the ken of the mortal)Every kiss regarding different relations bears magnanimity. As a mother kiss acquaints a subconscious mind and a newborn child with love. And since then this love begets a tie of motherly love. It gives him or her the first entrance into the majestic world of love. Thus a father kiss gives a birth to a tie of fatherly love; kiss of a brother imparts bondage of brotherly love; a friend's kiss makes a friendly bondage; a lover kiss makes a lovely-tie between two hearts and so on. This way the majesty of kiss is judged in the light of pure knowledge so its activity will be far-off extent. A kiss is nothing but a fragmentary sign or an instance of love. Thus kiss brings the heavenly bliss or an extreme happiness in life. Besides, it is the most popular sign of love. A kiss serves like a measuring-touchstone to test love being responded by the five organs of sense. In the absence of visible kiss an invisible kiss (i.e. a kiss of consciousness) makes life so romantic. Throughout life this kiss exists both in visible and invisible way. So life looks vigorous and pleasant. Irrespective of age it leaves a deep impression upon the conscious and subconscious mind, and showers down the heavenly bliss on them. And its hidden sublime force influences the mind. After all, if a kiss could not beget bliss or extreme happiness in life this beautiful creation would never be possible and love would be elusive. So, to get the lofty destination and the heavenly bliss in this mundane life kiss is the first trace.

However little, a kiss is stronger and more active than a painkiller, because may alleviate the pain of a distinctive part of a body, and its span of activity does not last for long time, but a kiss a prolonged influence upon an agonized mind. A kiss is the media for exchanging of sweetness of mind of this corporeal body. So this corporeal body seems a real media for love. If you observe ins and outs you must grasp that without a kiss of love no living being is blessed with the bliss of heaven. So, to exist a prolonged pleasure in life your love must be deeper and more profound, so your kiss will be blissful. It is very much sad that being the best creation by God you are abstain from such bliss! Everybody should remember a few good words; firstly, one should try utmost to awaken one's sense organs with one's deep and spontaneous kiss of love being inspired in and saturated with my mind and knowledge. A sweet bud opens its dreamy eyes with the kiss of breeze and the sun's light. Always one keeps in mind that a kiss of mind is sweeter than the kiss of with two lips; and a kiss of consciousness is the sweetest while consciousness becomes wakeful amid invisible feeling. Since then love becomes lively in the midst of kissing, and heavenly bliss descends the earth amidst this corporeal body. Besides, secrecy is the key to love. So a secret kiss is always sweet, because a kiss of consciousness is always secret and invisible.

Mind is so mysterious and abstruse to pry into it. Accordingly the worldly sense it is seen that—the more relation is deep, the more secrecy is deep, except blood relations. But, in wide outlook, the secrecy is the deepest while the relation becomes the deepest; and then the bliss comes down along with a kiss like a subterranean flow of a stream in this cursed life.

So the majesty or the magnanimity of a kiss is too profound to reach it. Kiss is a substitute for bliss, and bliss is a substitute for love. So kiss, bliss and love have coincided together with one another in this corporeal human body to beautify and sweeten the creation. In this respect I hope it will not be exaggerate that a single visible kiss is substitute for ten painkillers, and a single invisible kiss is substitute for hundred painkillers. When your intuition will respond to the call of soul will be loaded with love. You may get lots of bliss and enjoyment both through visible and invisible kiss. My friends, what do you yearn for? Do you not expect such a kiss to usher in the spontaneous bliss of heaven in your frustrated life? Whether you long for or not, it is your personal matter whether you desire such kiss or not where I have no entrance! So I stop here leaving the whole expected matter on your wise consideration!

EIGHTH CHAPTER

PROPER ACQUAINTANCE BEGETS LOVE

Life is a meaningful matter

Through proper acquaintance,

Nothing is better, all bitter

Without true consciousness

I welcome my readers of all classes irrespective of caste and creed. It seems that the whole of the world is immersing into the utter cry of distress and emptiness. Day after day people are becoming self-centered. Every heart is lamenting for a pang of separation. But why? Such question is now to all. But in spite of knowing it seems to be unknown to us. As if we are on avoiding this. Thus we are losing our-selves in the caver of the endless emptiness. Despite feeling we don't take care of this matter. You must astonish if you look at the dawn of the vast universe. Who are you? What is your acquaintance? And what are we doing every moment? If you can coincide your daily routine of your duty with your acquaintance, you feel stunned yourself. Are you right in your work as to your real acquaintance? Thus if you think of and judge, you will be able to understand what difference you are creating between your duty and your acquaintance. Thus degree-by-degree a disparity is automatically augmenting in your personal life. And this difference and disparity is about to touch upon the family, even social life along with your individual life. As a result a deep gap is on originating in humanity from man to man.

From this gap, an endless disparity in life is creeping up and begets the endless emptiness in this vast world. It is menacing the world peace also. And its sequel causes pride, vanity and jealousy that come about a gruesome war in the inner world of mind. Do you now want to save this beautiful life from this colossal war? Do you not hope for a beautiful and peaceful world? Of which every life will flourish? Do you not desire to dream of a beautiful and happy future generation through the building up of your own personal life? Perhaps, you may think that peace of world is relying only on you. No, always you have to remember that a family consists of man, a society is made of families, then state, even the world family. If you are not able to eradicate the germ of the disease of suffering and disappointment from your mind, it will not be possible for you to think of a beautiful life. To eradicate the germ of such frustration and disappointment from your mind you have to take Love-pill. Under its profound impact you will be able to cure these germs of diseases and will make you feel fresh and pleasant for living a peaceful life. If you can have fresh mind so you must feel a world of joy in life.

Your fresh mind then begets fresh thought of building up a house both in your personal and your family life; at once it will be turned into the thought of world family.

I think you must have understood what I have wanted to expatiate. I wish to touch upon it a little yet. It is sure that our great acquaintance is 'man'. It may be both male and female and 'man' is called the best of all creations in this vast world. So no animal is superior to man. Here is the question; no man knows what little duty he will be able to accomplish regarding his proper acquaintance. In this vast world whenever you will give your acquaintance, your proper acquaintance will be 'man'. And from this great acquaintance we get a lot of petty and inferior acquaintances. Every man enters the family from his personal life. So, the great acquaintance thus begets many fragmentary acquaintances in every individual life. So, everybody should try to evaluate the fragmentary acquaintance respecting one's great acquaintance. And if you want to establish yourself both in personal life and family life with fragmentary acquaintance you need love. Without love it is not possible to judge the fragmentary acquaintance. Always you have to think that this fragmentary acquaintance makes a bridge from mind to mind. But nobody will be possible to build up this bridge among the minds without tie of love. At first you have to be a right occupant of the abode of mind. Mind is your main provenance of love. Your first and foremost duty will be to cure your mind of any inhuman germ. Whatever acquaintances you are gathering in your personal life, concerning any fragmentary acquaintance, are your relations? These will come in to being and call for the proper action. Such acquaintance begets a bridge of love not only in specific boundary of life but out of the personal life. Hence one may haunt without any hesitation and frustration hundred minds and enjoy immense peace amid several acquaintances. To keep such acquaintances one must maintain proper duty accordingly one's real acquaintance.

Suppose, your acquaintance with your wife is husband, with your children you are a father, with brother and sister, you are a brother. Thus you may procure a good number of acquaintances, even out of your family. Man will be acquainted with different fragmentary acquaintances. With your lady—love, you are a lover, with your co—passenger of the same train, car and boat etc. you are like a friend, thus you are gathering a lot of fragmentary acquaintances throughout life and all these acquaintances give birth to many new relations. Thus you are endowed with many relations. But what little can you coincide your specific relation with your duty?

In this respect, such relations demand some distinct duties and every duty is vested with a few special characteristics. After all, whole matter depends on you. So, to keep consistency with your expected relation in respect of any distinguishable acquaintance you need fresh and open mind. In order to beautify your personal life for every moment you need love pill. Then whatever problem you face, you must overcome with fresh and delighted mental courage.

If the mind is endowed with hesitation and frustration, one finds it difficult to do overcome any problem.

Despite much strength and money one will not be able to approach any solution of any difficulty. One is the main foe of oneself and will become a meaningless thing to one self. So, one should drive all ailments and wants away from one's mind, so that no dearth or want can touch one's mind, because every mind is now suffering from the want of courage. Thus the want of self-confidence shatters the peace of personal life. It is real that one who loses self-confidence death haunts there always. So self-consciousness and self—confidence among people can be kept intact only with help of love pill as a panacea; it can bring about a colossal revolution in a man's mind and can make him healthy and courageous killing all germs of inhumanity and makes him think of a beautiful life and the world where man can live peacefully. Whenever you wish to mix with others (i.e. both male and female) amid your fragmentary relations, the others must demand a specific love accordingly your fragmentary relations. If you can respond truly to the call of them, you will feel a great pleasure for presence of true tie of love. But if you are not able to respond properly to this true acquaintance, and you wear a false acquaintance, there your acquaintance cannot expect any hopeful return from love, because love can't be nurtured by any pretext and falsity.

As to love, you are conscious of what I intend to say. If you want to be a happy man and desire to hug a happy isle of life, and to make others happy, please, since today you exert yourself to unveil your mask of falsity from your all-fragmentary acquaintances. One must feel an unuttered thrilling in one's mind. Whenever you'll tinge your any tiny acquaintance with probity your feeling will be teemed with a heavenly bliss. Based on the flawed acquaintance you never build any relation. By the response of one's unspoken heart and consciousness one should go ahead of making hundred of relations with others. So, both your personal and family life will be wonderful and beautiful. Each fragmentary acquaintance procreates a 'relation' and this relation is vested with love. Here love acts just like the sun. Wherever you go there is the sun. Even if you observe a very tiny place/cavern/pot etc. there you will find a ray of the sun. Like it a ray of light of endless love must lighten any relation resulting from human heart. It is obvious that no relation can grow up without love. So any relation is a minute part of the great love

NINTH CHAPTER

LOVE IS THE BEST CATALYST IN LIFE REACTION

Life is a protracted reaction

Love accelerates this action,

As a prolonged process

It keeps continuous access

Keeping an eye on a scientific aspect I am desirous of explicating this topic regarding love. How love has dissipated its influence in life and has regulated the whole of internal activities of life associated with both body and mind, but it remains always as impartial. The impartiality reminds me of a scientific issue called 'catalyst which is used in the chemical reaction to happen the chemical reaction faster and also reduces. But it remains unchanged throughout the reaction in spite of involving by itself in the reaction. Concerning this point, it is evident that life is also a prolonged reaction. And this whole reaction is still occurring under the influence of love. Here love acts as a catalyst.

Every life is embroiling in a prolonged reaction. This reaction goes on till death, because life is not free from anxiety, sorrow, pain and frustration. Sometimes life seems as fresh as a sunny morning, but occasionally it is gloomy and dull like a cloudy sky. Because life is loaded with ups and downs—regarding body and mind. Life frequently gets immersed in the largest reaction like a chemical reaction being collaborated with body and mind, where body consists of five primary elements namely earth, water, heat, air and space, and "mind" is called an internal organ. This mind is superimposed on ten organs, five organs of perception and five organs of action. There "mind" is above all these ten organs. So, love is playing its vital role in the reaction of life like a catalyst. Love remains unchanged. It regulates all activities in this reaction. As long as this reaction continues, love acts like a 'catalyst'. This reaction in life does not carry on its function smoothly and spontaneously in absence of love like catalyst.

So, I request you, my friends, to take this love in your life like a 'catalyst' to keep on speed up both your physical and mental action at every step of your worldly life. Because life means 'force,' and this 'force' comes into effect through 'attraction', and this attraction needs 'reaction'. Truly speaking, every moment in life is nothing but 'reaction'. To accelerate this reaction in a proper way love must be applied like a catalyst once you are able to love lovingly, so you find that your all activities in your life relating to mind, the best of all sense organs, will be manipulated by love like catalyst. I don't know what little I offer to your thirsty heart, and what little you accept it in your life. I believe that you will cherish 'love' like a catalyst in your life reactions. So, every reaction must turn into a new creation, which will fill your vacant heart.

TENTH CHAPTER

LOVE IS ENERGY

Love is a true energy

That is constant,

Whatever it possesses

Turned an eternal instant.

I welcome you from any corner of this vast world irrespective of caste, creed and manner to rouse your latent love of which unseen energy, power and force has kept you speed up and energetic. With its cryptic influence of beauty you look beautiful, with its profound suavity you are delighted and pleasant, and with its constant shower of blessing you are happy and peaceful. Without it you are a meaningless. You are requested to awaken your sleeping 'love' that lies in the very bottom of yourself and is going to be shrouded in ignorance. You don't delay a little—if you wish to be a real seeker after peace and a happy life, you must quest for occurring revolution of love. You should remember that without revolution of love in life you will not be able to free your mind from iniquities which are still fighting against the truth. You should judge your love in the light of humanity because your proper acquaintance is 'human'. You are still belonging to the family of human being. You never relinquish this 'quality' because it is your first and foremost 'pride' without which you are a good-for-nothing. It is your prime designation. If you neglect it you will be reattributed by your own essence and with the sting of conscience.

So, you should express your love through 'humanity'. It is your first duty; because, of course you never ignore your active life. Whenever one who refuses to do one's duty under anyone, he will be sacked from his duty or will be punished. Just like your prime duty is to respond to the call of the others accordingly your first quality 'humanity'. Without humanity you are just like a student without study. Being a human your first 'study' must be about humanity. Please you think, are you not a student without study? If it is; so our sequel must be dark and precarious. The essence is also associated with 'humanity'. Please you ask to yourself! You try your best to get a real answer, how it is possible by you to embrace a happy and a peaceful life. Remembering this, your essence is also crowned with 'humanity'.

Wherever do you live in? It is not my question to you. I want to say that you are going on frittering and humiliating your 'energy'. As a result you are becoming day-by-day a dependent. You are still becoming a doll in the hands of the others. As a man you are depriving you essence. Because, as a student without study, he is bound to depend on the other students having lost his

SANKAR SARKAR

own existence of studentship; you have also become like that. If you look around you must understand and realize how many beautiful lives are getting lost into the utter ugliness of inhumanity.

You are again requested to ponder over this expected issue. You don't lose your 'energy'. Don't be a weak. This world is not for the weak. You utmost try to sustain and maintain your love like energy. You should be a devotee to such love, which must provide you with an immense energy to go ahead of facing and confronting any difficulty at every step of your life. You nourish your 'love' in the abode of humanity'. If you attend upon "love", "love" must attend upon you in your any distress in the course of your worldly life.

If you think from your personal life to family life and from the family to the social life and from social life to the state life and so on you will be conscious of the havoc change in respect of humanity that goes on from the worse to the worst. Under such circumstances how it is feasible to proliferate and sprout your love-seed in such inconvenient ambience of inhumanity. If you look ahead, you must grasp and sketch your portrait of next days to which you are approaching. Perhaps, you must be deprived of your all energy to reach your destination, because you are still arrogant and obdurate to fulfill your egoism. But you have not a little time to think of your true essence. you have nothing but ugly 'egoism'— and day after day you are accustomed to addict to such 'egoism' or egoistic energy that has not a little meaning in reality of your essence. Such egoistic energy leads you to the hell, not to the heaven. it makes you forget your real essence and turns you into a dependant and destitute state.

Always you should be aware of two aspects one is 'bad' and other is 'good'. Whenever you will attempt to avoid your real course in life, the 'bad' qualities will be dominant and energetic, because you try to do against the proper response to your each organ of 'perception' and action'. Since then there must be fighting between 'the good' and 'the bad'. as a result, you are still on dilemma' because you are mainly responsible for such frustrated outcome. You are stubborn and affront against your true path and direction to which you have been led by supreme order. You are 'you', and you are still blessed with your true essence against which power you are ignoring constantly.

My friends! I intend to discuss that 'energy' what you feel continuously in yourself and keeps you energetic and delighted. it is nothing but a fragmentary energy of the enormous energy called "love". It is also called "individual energy" which has come of 'love'. It has no ending and destruction. Even it cannot be created and ruined. I hope my readers must be delighted and pleasant in accordance with my expected explication on the basis of Law of conservation of energy by a great scientist, Isaac Newton concerning the expected subject.

You may ask why I intend to quote the scientific law in respect of discussing 'love'. I expect it will be very easy task for me to lighten highly the matter of love clearly for your parched heart we are still in the age of science. We are too sophisticated to understand anything without scientific logic. Especially for the devotees of science, I shall be able to bring out a ray of deep delineation regarding love. How love is omnipotent, being a weeny part of such omnipotence we are still ignorant of its singularity. Accordingly this world renowned Scientific Law, 'energy' has no 'mass', even it is invisible. And it can't be touched but feeling only. Love is like that 'energy'—it can be only perceived but unseen; it can't be touched with any mortal finger and limb. Only its existence can be felt and discerned with the organs of perception. Even 'energy' is also perceptible. As 'energy' can be changed from one aspect to another, but it does not lose its essence, namely it never gets damaged or destroyed. Any 'energy' is also perceptible. Any 'energy', however little, can't be destroyed and created in anyway. it remains omnipresent. Without 'energy' both the animate and the inanimate world are non-existent. Here is a best question in respect of such discussion regarding 'energy'—if you think deeply; it will be manifest to you that 'energy' is perceived and felt by any living being, whenever both the animate and the inanimate come so close to each other. 'Energy' wholly depends on its manipulation. It needs a distinct media whenever something is called 'energy', it indicates somewhat 'individually.'

'Love' is a great 'energy' in every life. Without this energy life is inactive and seems to be a handicapped. Here is also a good aspect of explanation as to 'love' that is the main source of all 'energy'. The idea of energy through feeling, perception and discernment by a living being is appreciated. But a 'man' is the best 'being' to have its profound perception. Now, if you judge it consciously and keenly the real quality of anything can be discerned fully with the help of the same quality of same thing. Here the quality of any energy is perceived in a full-fledged by any media (i.e. both animate and inanimate) endowed with energy. Here to have a subtle importance of energy human being is a proper media because 'human being' is associated with different types of energy collectively. so, any distinctive and separate energy are possible for a man to feel easily because man is implanted with vast energy. And any 'energy' yields to it.

Carefully listen to what I intend to tell, my friend! Whatever is in this vastness is also present in this mortal frame on the basis of the knowledge of the immortal soul. Please, try your best to realize-this human body consisting of five elements out of which this vast world is not possible. Individually 'the energy' of every distinct element co-exists in a human body, but it gets a conscious life whenever other three perceptible elements come in contact with this mortal body (i.e. mind, understanding and pride). Such distinguishable energy of each elements collectively turning into a great attraction which has also turned into a purified name 'Love', this mortal human body is the best media of "love". Here it is conspicuous that 'love' begets thousands of distinctive energy. out of this love any individual energy is spiritless. If you think directly or indirectly, the sun is the main source of all energy in the external world, love is also the main source of all energy or power regarding the inner world of a human life; even in the widest sense, love is the source of all energy or power regarding the world of living being. Now I discuss an interesting matter in accordance with love. As energy changes its place and media accordingly the media and place it exhibits its essence; but it remains unchanged internally in respect of its true essence. "Love" is just like energy. It only changes media. Considering its expected media, it displays its true essence. And it is sure that its media is overwhelmed with its energy. Without this energy every media with a specific name becomes meaningless and lifeless. Suppose, a mortal frame is conceived by any specific or distinct media "man" is named in this family 'father' or 'mother' or 'brother' and so on. In respect of a man's distinct acquaintance love like energy makes him or her spirited, and also keeps him or her in motion. But it is a matter of thinking that same 'love like energy' accordingly media changes its external characteristic regarding distinctive relation. If you put a little water in a pot, it takes the shape of this pot; just like 'love' also takes also the media's shape in respect of inner way.

Truly speaking, love is a proper energy in life. Without its unseen presence life is dead. So everybody ought to enhance his inclination towards love. and he is asked to tend and cherish love cordially in his mind; if you want to get the proper result of love you have to manipulate yourself in a proper way. It is true that if you apply everything properly in this world you must get a distinctive result from your applied thing (i.e. both animate and inanimate). Why not? You must have a good result from love. if you utilize or apply it in your life accordingly its subtle characteristics, Love must beget its 'energy' with which influence you must dwell in the state of enthusiasm. Always you have to remember that every living being is blessed with specific energy that attracts with one another. Especially human life is so distinctive and fresh. so every human life is the best for responding to another unseen or unspoken call of energy spontaneously. So a life yearns after responding to others. and thus a profound inclination, attraction, affinity and affection are created. if you judge this matter of the deep thought regarding love in the light of consciousness and knowledge and intelligence, this obscure matter will be clear and transparent. You are told to be aware of such attraction or attachment between two hearts or lives or minds. here such attraction means 'energy', and this 'energy' is nothing but a purified or sacred name 'love'. Many a time I have discussed that love expresses itself accordingly media. It is love that makes a beautiful bondage between two brothers. Such a bondage of 'energy' called 'fraternity'. Here this word 'fraternity' is nothing but 'energy or power' that's purified name of love, in this way there are thousand types of 'bondages' are making from life to life or heart to heart, such as between a lover and a beloved, a mother and father, a daughter and a father so on. If you think calmly and deeply you must realize that such 'bondage' between two hearts from man to man in accordance with different media the 'energy' or 'power' means love, which displays in a winding course of human life. Hope you have grasped what I have intended to explain. That is very much exigent in course of your life, even at every step of your life for a while. It is such 'energy' or 'power' by which you are going ahead and making a bridge from heart to heart, and you are also crossing the bridge of every moment in your active life. Is it possible for you to pass the curious moment without 'energy' or 'power' in your life?

If not! Why you are not accustomed to devoting yourself to sustain this 'energy' or 'power' in your life? Why are you wasting this energy in vain? Always you have to keep in mind that the misuse of your true 'energy' of your own essence makes your life miserable and abject. Where you live, there you are still chained with a specific relation, which makes 'bondage' between two hearts. this bondage of relation comes into effect through an energy or power. after all, such 'bondage' of hearts is nothing but a 'energy' or 'power' or 'force' that's called love.

If you are not able to apply and maintain such energy or power regarding media in your life, you never expect a good result from such 'energy or power'. It is obvious that having lost such 'energy' or 'power' you are becoming day after day weak, feeble, and inactive. You feel frustration and hopelessness in every sphere of your life. It goes without saying that "a sound health begets a sound mind"—So, in wider sense we are still a man of unsound mind with unsound health. As a result, we are getting deprived of it in every walk of life. Our aim ends and desire never reaches any fixed destination. The word 'love' is a 'bondage' that means an attraction' which is nothing but 'energy' or power. It sustains this bondage. However little, it is amongst the whole of population of this vast world. It has also occupied every turn of the life and is above all. We neglect it so we have become the disregarded ones to this true energy or 'power'. And an inauspicious energy or power destroys our life gradually. We are unsuccessful in every battle of our life. If you think you must grasp this matter that we are inferior to a beast. You should try to enlarge and expand this love like energy more and more having sustained this energy in you and try to be a brave to confront any obstacle. You should try to get back your golden throne in the question of 'love' on the ground of your real acquaintance 'humanity'. I have thrashed out the energy. now I intend to acquaint you with its diversified aspect. I hope you are already accustomed to the transformation of energy. It is true that 'energy' can be transformed from the one place to another, but it does not lose its existence. If you think this matter so profoundly you must realize how 'energy' plays the key role in every sphere of your daily life all over this world. Whatever 'energy' may be, especially 'energy' remains invisible and unseen. It lightens and strengthens the other thing. Remaining unseen it makes other thing visible. You have to remember that 'the sun' is the main source of all energy in this world. Without blessing of the sun nothing comes into effect in the outside world concerning energy.

Like that, 'love' is the main source of energy of the inner world of life. Love like energy' has also many a form in respect of different fields in this human life. Every life is crowned with individual and true energy without which life can't be thought properly. As a man you apply this 'energy' in your every turn of active life and you may get progress continuously. The sun keeps the outside world alive with its invisible energy. In the way love-like Sun keeps alive the inner world. And its energy elevates and lightens the ins and outs of the inner world. In this respect, love means supreme energy, and the main source of all energy regarding inner activities of this human life. Every human life is a suitable media that is saturated with its part of energy. Regarding this you are nothing but a tiny part of this love-like supreme energy. If you mind, you may solve any hard problem in your daily life, even throughout your life utilizing this energy, which has been implanted into you. Such 'energy' has also many forms. If necessary, you may transform this 'energy' into different forms to accomplish you ends. Always you should cherish in mind that the whole of the human family seems still alive owing to existing this energy into them. In panoramic outlook, all living beings are subject to this energy. Suppose, you are a father in your family; this word 'father' would be meaningless and valueless without 'energy'; such 'energy' makes you 'father' from 'man' to which you still belong. Again you may transform your 'fatherly energy' into 'brotherly energy.' 'Love energy', 'Friendly energy' and so on, but you are still unchanged in your real essence of energy. You may transform this into different energies amid the modification of your true 'energy' of love. In course of discussion, perhaps you may have a question in this context why I have discussed about 'fatherly energy', 'brotherly energy' and friendly energy and so on. What do I want to mean by it? Why such type of question is arising here? Please, let me acquaint its hidden significance with you! I hope you must fathom it. Whenever you have opened your two eyes and have looked about you in course of time on the basis of flourishing of your latent knowledge, you'll find yourself among a lot of relations, and you will go on feeling a singular amusement. If you cogitate deeply having enhanced your subtle feeling it will be very much comprehensible to you; because every 'relation', in your life means a kind of 'bondage'. Without this bondage you can't go ahead a single step. But this 'bondage' means an attraction' between two lives, or from life to life in respect of several relations. This 'attraction' means a sort of 'energy' which attracts a life with one another and makes such bondage'. But such 'energy' is a part of love-like supreme energy. It invisibly makes an eternal bondage between the life and the world. We feel an unseen and unspoken attraction for this beautiful world. So man can't do anything, and can't move an inch without blessing of this 'energy'. Generally we can't observe the entity and essence of this energy easily. We are not able to appreciate this energy. We are unaware and unconscious of our true essence. we are ignorant and blind of feeling and thinking of any profound matter relating to this life.

However, it is obvious that you are able to bring peace and happiness in your life applying this 'energy' in your course of life. It helps you to solve any problem if you utilize this 'energy' properly. You may feel energetic, and enjoyable in the every turn of your dutiful life by dint of this 'energy'. In absence of this 'energy' you are energy less and hopeless and frustrated fragment of this vast living world. So you should first become a devotee to this love-like supreme energy while feeling the essence of this energy since then you must be able to surmount any suffering, and frustration from your life with the help of this latent 'energy'. Then you feel and live always in a peaceful mood. Naturally a young boy attracts for a beautiful young girl. If you discern deeply you must understand that an unseen or invisible 'energy' begets such attraction between two hearts. And bondage is made between them' such 'attraction' may come into effect between them due to several causes or reasons' but such reasons are not out of five organs of perception, five organs of action led by the inner organ "mind". Always you have to keep in mind that essence of your life exists in true energy that is a part of love-like supreme energy. Whenever you desire to accustom yourself to the wrong way of 'energy' instead of the true, it leads gradually you to a destructive way' and frustration and disappointment must befall on you. So, it is a matter of thinking to be kept in mind that 'love' is a beautiful, sacred and heavenly attraction between two hearts, but you never forget that this attraction is made by 'energy' without which you are non-existing. So, my friend, you try your best to strengthen your heart's bondage with other. Then you will feel an immense 'energy' to make a life without frustration and despair. And this 'energy' makes your mind courageous and inspired to think spontaneously of any arduous subject, which seems to be useful to your life.

ELEVENTH CHAPTER

LOVE IS THE GREATEST INSPIRATION

To sustain this world productive

Love acts as a great inspiration,

Devoid of love like action

Life becomes a bit of emotion,

Who does not want to make his own life purposeful? In order to make your life purposeful you are working hard in a constant manner. You are so busy with your active life. But despite toiling much you are not able to make your life purposeful and reach your fixed destination. Why? Have you pondered over this matter? Though you are investing much labour and time, your purpose is turning into ashes in the long run. If you take a broad view regarding your life, it will be clear to you that some reasons of deficiency are too dominant in your life to fulfill your purpose. To do fulfill any desire and purpose in life 'courage' is very much essential; but what type of 'courage' has been invoked here. A life is associated with two types of 'courage'—one is 'mental courage' and other is 'physical courage'. Here 'mental courage' is very indispensable. Because of deficiency of proper 'mental courage' most people are not able to make their life purposeful. Such 'deficiency' is engulfing a good number of people in every family and society. So such family and society face it difficult to make it purposeful; because 'a man' is the life of this vast family. Without your presence in person you never think of the existence of this vastness in a wider sense. So at first you should free yourself from the reasonable deficiencies to make your life purposeful. As to this, you are asked to see about your own deficient plight that prevents you from thinking of a purposeful life. So, it is evident that 'courage' and 'inspiration' are substitute for each other. Based on the discussion, if you think deeply, you will see that you still suffer from deficiency of 'inspiration.' Its deficiency can make your life a desert and aimless and without proper inspiration you will be not able to inspire your inner constituent elements which have been carrying prime roles to make your life purposeful; because you are non-existent without them. Suppose, a 'wristwatch' consists of various instruments, without these instruments the wristwatch has no value, as much as it frame looks very beautiful. Man uses the wristwatch to know time. If not, man would never use this wristwatch so much its inner shape may be splendid. Like it, 'you' are nothing but a 'frame of man' without proper activity of your inner constitutes. So, always you should keep in mind that your 'desire' and 'wish' should be relevant to the unspoken purpose of your inner constituents, which collectively and covertly buttress all 'wishes' and 'purposes' amid you. Here you are a mere media. I hope that you have understood my subject matter what I have intended to bring before you. You will feel an inexplicable pleasure whenever your purpose or desire will be inspired by the unuttered response to the inner constituent elements of your own self or by others. But it is very hard to be inspired by one self. Man finds it very difficult to sustain his life smoothly if the loneliness grows in haste. As social being we need companion. In this respect, I want to speak of a few words that seem to be very useful to your life. Wherever you live you will see that you get involved yourself in the bondage or the relation by an unseen attractive force. When any relation responds to your mind under the influence of such unseen force, it is turned into the name of love. And such love begets a proper immense inspiration to inspire you for making your life purposeful. For want of proper inspiration from proper media one's inner constituents remain uninspired. (Here inner constituents, ten organs of perception and action and an internal organ, mind). So, the more you strengthen the tie of love, the more you will get inspiration. If everybody should remember that an uninspired life can't be fruitful and complete. Before I have told that this inspiration comes of two sources—one is your 'own self', and the next is 'the others'. But it is very hard to be inspired by one self; because we all are social beings. However, one should know that love is the greatest inspiration to inspire one's life to sustain the active life smooth. Thus if you think, you must grasp that 'inspiration only can give birth to a lot of new creations through life. To get such inspiration you must build up a strong bondage of love with which you are still living. An invisible force relates us with one another. Whenever you will feel the absence of this invisible force, you feel deserted and exiled. And an uttered loneliness and isolation kills your greenness of the mind. All the time you believe that—an inspired life is just like a hydrogen balloon that soars up gradually. The span of a life is a collection of thousand moments; so without moment the life can't be thought in the question of its existence. To sweeten your every turn in your dutiful life you need a true inspiration. Every inspired moment can bring in your life a new aspect of hope and make your life purposeful.

Always you should keep a deep liaison with them those who are still standing closely to the door of your mind—namely the members of your family, particular persons and friends who are soothing your tiring hours day after day Because they are the main sources of your inspiration. As to relation, you may build up many a bridge of love to haunt easily from mind to mind. So, to get smooth and spontaneous life your love also must be spontaneous and candid towards others. Then their unasked inspiration will impart to you a lot of pleasures to make your life purposeful. When your constituents do not get inspired, they stop responding to and losing its capacity for providing you inspiration or courage. In order to develop and make your life purposeful inspiration plays the key role to activate your inner compositions specially organs of perceptions and mind. So love is thicker than blood. Based on love, any relation can inspire you more than any other relations, though it is not blood relation. So you are requested to 'inspire' your every moment of your life to enliven and beautify your every desire and purpose. Mind that, your ninety nine percent hard work is equal to one percent inspiration. If you are always bereft of such inspiration, your ninety-nine percent hard work will be turned into ashes. At this matter you ought to be conscious of each fragmentary 'inspiration' resulting from any source. This inspiration may lead your life to a new course. So you should not ignore any 'inspiration', however little it may be, because without love no inspiration comes into being. You should try your best to expose yourself to your close ones for whom you are still on working hard and feeling strength like courage When you are getting love, however little, from your close-one in return for your love is really called 'inspiration'. It ushers a new and purposeful consciousness to your curious mind. Since then your life feels plenty of rejoice. In this respect, you may get a lot of burning examples if you observe how man relinquishes his hope and desire of his life for want of a little inspiration. However petty, it acts just like a spark of fire, and also a little contact of a piece of touchstone. You never forget that love begets this inspiration. Love is the prime source of it. The more your rivulet of love gets ebbed, the more your stream of inspiration will be dried up. So you must quote this in your mind that love is your capital, inspiration is its interest, for you should try your heart and soul to increase in the worth of love to get enough inspiration to cheer up every turn of your life. A student can brighten and succeed his main purpose of his life (i.e. education) when his teacher inspires him. A lover does not hesitate to take any risk in his life whenever his beloved inspires him and so on. Thus different relevant names regarding your relationship with different persons may appear in your life; and you may have a lot of inspirations from various sources in proportion to your love towards them. As a few drops of dew can cause the sweet sleeping bud bloom, as inspiration can enhance and flourish your all-latent faculties of your perceptive organs, which can lead you to a purposeful destination. So, as love begets inspiration and inspiration begets true courage for facing any obstacle to fulfill your purposeful life. A life without inspiration is full of hopelessness, because an uninspired life gets immersed into despondency and emptiness. So you should commit to memory that you are a slave to love. Love is not slave to you. We are always in favour of love. A man who works under your leadership for a few hours, he always wants to satisfy you with his utmost endeavour, and you also expect that he should work accordingly you. If he is after your mind, you must please with him and may engage him in another work. You don't forget that you are like a slave or servant to love. You should try utmost to get its favour, otherwise you will be sacked from the getting of pleasure and enjoyment of your active life. Now I desire to tell you a few words as to 'inspiration' without which your life is shattered. So, I shall request you to keep an item concerning 'inspiration' in your daily menu of your busy life, so that you may get a plentiful power or energy to activate your exhausted organs to make them active. Suppose, you are a healthy, strong and a handsome man you have enough wealth. So you are a happy man outwardly; but you are a weak and frustrated forlorn. Internally you are really unhappy. Why? Have you asked yourself? So, you have omitted the item of 'inspiration' from your everyday menu of your life. This deficiency has made you a frustrated chap. You should remember that only true 'inspiration' could bring back a true consciousness to your shattered or exhausted life. And this consciousness must be concomitant with knowledge, which will help you to steer your life. If you are requested to dive into the very depth of your knowledge there you must find, that without inspiration nothing has been possible. You will face several obstacles and hindrances that prevent you from reaching your lofty position. To surmount such problems you need the 'inner force', which only comes from 'Inspiration'. And you should think that love is the greatest cause of the creation of your inspiration. Even there has been a hidden mystery of 'inspiration' behind any creation of this vast universe. I have no wish to puzzle you with this thinking of the vastness. I only wish you to think of yourself, so that you may be able to make your life spontaneous inspired by yourself or by your all close-ones. So, the more you love, the more you will get inspiration. Only love can meet your all wants and dearth of your life. So I intend to remind you of an important speech that—inspiration is the first and foremost incarnation for any new creation in life. Until inspiration can awaken your dormant consciousness from the state of sub consciousness, your perceptive organs and mind will not be able to perceive the interest in and pleasure for taking a new creative step in thinking of any new matter in perspective of every precious moment of your life. After all, if you want to spend your life freed from frustration, you have to take inspiration in your mind every moment. So every inspired moment can make your life momentous. The more you will widen the scope of your love, the more 'inspiration' will inspire your life. Since then your life will look shining and bright in the midst of all sorrows and pains and struggles.

TWELFTH CHAPTER

LIFE AND LOVE ARE SUBSTITUTE FOR EACH OTHER

Where is love, there life is patent

Single of them seem to be latent.

In long journey time is a great steed

Love is its rider to keep its true speed.

I desire to give an emphasis on the manipulation of 'interest' (i.e. 'intention' 'desire') in this chapter regarding life. I intend to start with asking a question. If you are asked—Are you good at Math? If you are good at it; you must answer 'yes'! If not, so you will answer-'No'. It is a matter of thinking that generally whether you are good at your expected subject. In which subject one is more interested will be one's favourite subject. So without interest nothing comes into effect in life. There must be a distinct interest in order to do any work. Whenever one will take any interest in one's distinctive subject, one will long for that subject. And it will take root firmly in the very depth of one's own inclination. Day after day one's desire will grow for finding out more and the profound nuance of the specific subject. And this curiosity makes man more interested on the one hand; on the other hand it also makes man successful in discovering the singularity of his interest in expected subject. Since then you will be able to discover a new aspect, which brings you a world of joy. If not, nothing would come into being in this world. What you like best, at first, you should learn a lesson properly to grow your interest for that subject. Because proper interest in any subject begets a proper will for invention or discovery by man. Without interest nothing will be fruitful. In this respect, life is nothing but an interest in anything that keeps man ecstatic and pleasant always. So, one should keep in mind that fickle and weak interest in any subject can't make one a fulfilled. You will be apposite for getting proper pleasure and happiness in your life, because man's life is not out of a collection of interests. Every moment begets a distinctive interest in man's life. Whenever man eschews his interest regarding any expected matter, man starts feeling uneasy and discomfort. Thus your interest gets fallen back in your life for a long time, so you must face disappointment, and in the world of frustration enclosed by uneasy and bitter circumstances and incidents. On the ground of this discussion, one should remember that—The more one takes an interest in one's expected thing, the more one gets pleasure regarding that subject or thing or matter. Besides, the more knowledge extends regarding subject, the more interest grows proportionately.

One must acquire knowledge of one's expected subject to keep one's interest intact. Both knowledge and interest synchronize in life. To explore or discover any new thing and subject you must go to the very heart of nature. Perhaps, you must have understood why I have pointed out such a matter of discussion; you may have a question relating to this. I hope you have got your answer. Because, if your 'interest' is proper, and distinct accordingly your true desire of character. Such interest in any subject must make you a proper interested man. Since then your true interest leads you to a lofty position of joy and happiness. Then you get a profound and deep interest to increase your proclivity in your subject. You must have an intense knowledge of your subject matter. If you think deeply it will be clear to you that any inclination to and longing for a distinct subject begets a fragmentary 'interest'. So, always you have to remember that—the more one augments one's interest in one's respective subject, the more one will get pleasure. But, whenever you will enlarge or widen your interest in your fixed subject, your yearning must grow fast to get a panoramic knowledge of your specific subject. So from such discussion it is conspicuous that interest is the first and foremost matter in man's life. This 'interest' means inclination, tendency, proneness, desire and affection for and devotion to a fixed thing according to the disposition of the different men. Perhaps, you must grasp this matter that such 'interest' stands for a specific thing or matter or an subject. So these also stand for 'interest'. Such type of interest is like a fragmentary 'interest' of the great interest, for which the little interest exists in life. Both life and love coexist with each other when this life is regarded as the greatest subject and 'love is also the greatest 'interest' in life, Perchance, you have understood what I have wished to speak of the above discussion. When you will take this life like the best subject and will delve into the mystery and singularity of this subject you must have a deep interest in this said subject. Such 'interest' in a specific subject (i.e. 'life') is compared here to 'love'. If you want to develop your keen interest in love regarding life, your first duty is to know elaborately your subject called 'life'. If you don't widen the ken of your subject matter, you will be regardless. Here 'life' is regarded as a subject. In this case, love stands for life, and life stands for love. On this point, love and life is substitute for each other. It is a matter of curiosity that every life is just like an unknown new book coated with colorful cover written by God. If you give a little emphasis upon this displayed matter for realizing so, you may have an immense enlightenment in this respect. If not, man must be unaware and unconscious of life. Whenever you intend to go through a new book with rapt attention and delighted mind your mind will be anxious for knowing the incident after incident what have been equipped in order page after page. Like that, if man's life is also an unknown new book filled with miscellaneous mysterious events and incidents, so man's desire must rise up. For every moment men are gathering and coming across with new experiences, knowledge and ordeals through turning over pages after pages of these life like book. That 'interest' you are gathering reading these lives like unknown book is a true 'interest'. The more you develop this 'interest' in life like book, the more your mind will be curious for knowing the unknown. After all life is nothing but an unknown book which is shrouded in mysteries. So, man is so curious for it. It indicates that 'interest' (i.e. 'love') and life must coincide with each other. Broadly speaking, life is a blend of enormous fragmentary 'interests' collectively called 'love'. And these fragmentary interests resulted from different organs of action and perception including mind. So man cannot pass a little moment without interest (i.e. wish). Life seems then bitter and indignant whenever it is bereft of a singular "interest" in anything. Whenever your every moment is spent with pleasure or curiosity your life feels an unspoken interest or romance in everything. Such 'interest' is not out of love. After all with which 'interest' you pass every moment rejoice that is 'love'. And your 'tiny' and 'fragmentary interest' delighten your daily life resulting from love. Always one should think that an interested moment makes one's life bitter and frustrated. But 'an interested' moment makes one's life pleasant and romantic. So, one must try to pass every moment through an interest. However this fragmentary interest comes of love. Your life is nothing but the collection of moments. Your main duty is to sweeten every moment with a golden touch of love to live a peaceful life. My readers! I wish you to rouse your fragmentary interest or desire to know deeply the every incident of your life-like unknown book. If once you can augment your interest in your life-like book, so 'love' must open its golden door for your entrance. In this respect, it is said that pleasure and peace are vested in your own hand. The more you read your unknown life-like book, the more you have pleasure. So, you 'never kill your 'interest' in anyway regarding your life. To kill interest in any matter regarding life means to killing moment out of which life is non-existing. So you must be conscious of enlivening tiny 'interest' that keeps your life speedy

THIRTEENTH CHAPTER

LOVE IS A GLASS OF SORBET

Let the mind partake of love heartily

Let life think what she is properly

Let life forget the mundane tiredness

Let love consume all bitterness

Nobody can confine love to a fixed definition and a few words. Only the great men have given their distinguished opinions about love, because love is limitless. Love is endless, universal and boundless. It is as generous as sky, as bottomless as the ocean. It responds to the call of different people in different ways. Although it has no 'starting and 'ending' yet its invisible presence in every life is very much appreciated. It can't be seen with naked eyes but feeling. Only its unseen presence of power and force is felt and discerned. So, having come in contact with its golden touch, life becomes happy within its limited span.

As the image of the ocean can be assumed in a drop of water, the roar of the sea can be heard through the sound of a conch, even from a ray of light can be perceived of the great sun. just like, we can feel, visualize and discern the least presence of the boundless love within our sacred heart. So these beautiful and wonderful worlds are filling up with the heart rendering songs of the enraptured hearts of the great people by love's splendid touch. And age after age love fills thousand of empty hearts with its grandeur melody. So I welcome my all readers to take the tiny part of love to their heart and spend this dutiful and agonized life pleasantly and happily amid proper application in every sphere of life. You will be able to finish your worldly functions happily. Who does not want a happy and beautiful life? Who does not intend to pass every moment joyfully? So I request all classes of readers to rouse love in their hearts and try to appreciate its presence properly. So, every step of life will be fresh and shining like a sunny morning. The speed of life will be just like a flow of subterranean river. What little you are able to feel and discern of this great love will be enough for you to gain much felicity in your worldly life. Truly speaking, you will be then really a happy man.

Your heavy exhausted heart is overwhelmed with an unuttered ecstasy meeting your close ones. You forget all tiredness for a moment; even a ray of hopelessness can't leave a stain upon your face. So I again remind you of love, which is just, like a glass of sarbat to a tired body because, it can alleviate all exhaustion of body, though for a little time. If you can contain it (i.e. love) in your mind always, no tiredness of anxiety could touch you in spite of ups and downs of life. You never mix love with other things. Always keep in mind that love is entirely a matter of mind. It can be judged and felt intuitively and spontaneously. Despite its presence in every heart men are unconscious of its application. It is men's great fault for which men suffer from many problems in their life. I wish to cast a little light through my indigent discussion, please, listen to what I desire of enlightening about love. You are requested not to equalize love and sex.

Sex is very essential and indispensable in life, because without sex this beautiful creation is impossible. But, it is a matter of thinking that love never comes after sex. It is quite impossible to erect a castle of heavenly love on the pleasure of sex. it will be just like a temporary dam made of emotion. Because sex is based on body whose splendid beauty charms and allures sex. That beauty of body allures your sensitive organs is momentary, transient and mortal. What love comes into being through sex is a kind of sexual emotion that seems to be love, but really it is not love. Suppose, if the beauty of body for which you are mad to get is deformed by any natural or unnatural accident—will you like then that body? Since then your attraction for her or him will be shrunk. But, if you would try your best to get sexual happiness in the midst of love, then nothing can prevent you from approaching towards her or him because of the attraction between two hearts where true love still exists. Hence no external deformation of her or his body could make you hopeless.

So always you should cherish this thought that without love only sex is nothing but a pretext to indulge in getting physical pleasure. And if love begets sex then it will be a reason for a great joy. Despite understanding and grasping we are committing mistake continuously. Love first influences mind or heart, then pure and true mind decides whether sex is acceptable or not in this respect. Heart is the main source of influx of love. Love is always beyond catching and touching but visualizing and feeling and discerning. Everything needs a specific media without which nothing can express itself properly. Like that, heart is the proper media of invisible power of love. In the next chapter about 'media' is discussed, how media plays the key role in the arena of love.

If you mind you may have sexual pleasure with money, but there you can't have mental satisfaction. It is true that call-girl-offers her body to you for money but mind, which is hidden and covered with mystery, there you are not able to reach. So both you and she are not anxious to each other for an extreme mental satisfaction, besides, you can never compare your wife, beloved or any close ones with this call girl' 'I love my wife'—but you are not able to explain conspicuously, because you never ask to yourself, why do you love? How do you feel respecting her love? You feel astound in spite of remaining "love" in your heart. You never try to resuscitate your love, so long as it seems to be latent.

So, my friends don't delay more. Since now, even from this moment you promise to respond to your covert love what little exists in you. Do not forget that you are a 'man', and it is your great and prime acquaintance (Parichaya). Centering this acquaintance whenever you will enter the family from your personal life there you will acquire many acquaintances and every acquaintance will beget a new relation. Only you have to be conscious of manifesting your every relation through love. so you will realize that no complexity is arising, because a man can't spend a single day without company. There must be necessary any expected relation in life. This relation needs a sort of love. This love makes a liaison from heart to heart. About this elaborately will be discussed in the next part.

FOURTEENTH CHAPTER

LOVE IS GOD

Betwixt life and the world

Love occurs the co-existence,

God descends every heart

By ladder of consciousness

To prove its true existence

In this chapter I am going to thrash out Love and God. It is sure that this seems very hard subject yet I desire to throw a glimpse upon this expected subject. In this respect many a man has given various opinions and ideas and thoughts according to their own conscience. Some people have believed that God is omnipresent, omniscient and omnipotent. After all they adhere to this opinion that God has created this beautiful world. Again some believe that God is nothing but a bubble of ignorance called superstition. Some think that God is nothing, Nature is God. Some cogitate that God is the main source of energy of all creations; even some mind that 'God' is the unseen power, which seems supreme power that has been implanted by the creator called God. Besides, science merely believes in the existence of God. However, God may be! It is not my burning question. But my asking is here that-whoever you may be! Whatever your acquaintance may be! You may be a politician, historian, philosopher, economist, scientist, writer, poet, singer, composer, and farmer etc.—You are requested to think of your proper acquaintance from which you have got such many fragmentary acquaintances—about this I have discussed in the previous chapter. You are a 'man' which is your proper acquaintance, and having entered the small family in comparison with the vast family (universe) whatever acquaintance you have been endowed with are called fragmentary acquaintance'. And your first quality or manner or characteristic called humanity—Now you are asked to contemplate regarding your proper acquaintance on the basis of your first proper quality 'humanity', so, you may have not such type of controversial question relating to God! Because whatever God may be; in the question of your humanity if you ponder over 'existence', 'mind', 'heart' and "soul "—out of which you are non-existent. These are unseen and invisible things, which can be thought and realized on the basis of abstract ideas and knowledge. But without these 'life' can't be thought a bit. If you deeply ponder over this matter, perhaps you may get a suitable idea of this mystery regarding your 'existence' or 'essence'—how it is regulated! If you intend to construe your own 'essence', so you must realize that.

Whatever seems to be true and proper are invisible and mysteries. only it can be guessed, assumed, conjectured and realized on the abstract thought and philosophic ideas. That the sparkling of subtle energy influences your mind can be felt only—the provider or Surveyor or originator or creator of such subtle and sublime energy or power are regarded as God. As Science is a specific knowledge of anything amid practical application by a man who is not out of that 'mind' or 'heart' and 'soul' which begets proper knowledge coming in contact with anything under the influence of true consciousness, so the power or energy of your intuition lightens the other thing in the outside world—since then science comes into being. Is it not? In this way it is thought.

So it will be clear that—'essence' of every living being is associated with an invisible subtle energy or power that is nothing but the presence of expression of God's power. Only your subtle and beautiful belief can bring this feeling. My friends! I don't want to kill your precious time talking over the existence of God! So, I desire to say that whatever your think, or say with help of your true, beautiful, sacred and conscious 'mind', 'heart' & 'soul'—is the expression of God as the sun lightens all in the outside world, and God lightens the inner world. With respect to this discussion such a question may arise that—human being is too egoistic, pride and conservative to think broadly of the true essence of life. We are too sophisticated and modern to cogitate over the beauty of the inner world. We are so engrossed in the gross that we can't forsake the gross thought and can't superimpose the outside beauty on the inner beauty.

We are not perfect and can't possess that pure and sacred soul. As a result, we are not able to meet God face to face. Perhaps, a few sacred souls have got this heavenly opportunity, and they may have it. So you may feel God's presence amid love, because love itself is the truest expression of God. In this respect, God is the incarnation of love; and love is the incarnation of God. Where is love, there is God. Mind, heart and soul are invisible and inner organs grasped amid the abstract thought of truth, beauty and sanctity. So, the more you love, the more you realize or feel the existence of God in you. Whoever you may be—if you keenly discern, it will be obvious to you that the response of your consciousness must compel and guide you to go to the path of the truth; but such response is not possible in absence of love which is nothing but the self-expression of God himself. Without love your life seems lifeless and nonexistent. Love develops itself in a convenient atmosphere in the inner world of life. The essence of God also progresses in equal proportion to love. So, as everyman is endowed with love, everyman is also endowed with God; both love & God are substitute for each other. In accordance with this discussion, that life is so inclined to the gross-love is blind of existence of God. So man is not able to realize its nuance and equality, that love is nothing but the incarnation of God, and God is nothing but the true expression of love amid the animate, specially human being.

Such an invisible energy or force or power is the main source of reason of this vast creation. What is that energy, power and force? Who has contained this? The uncountable fragmentary energy or power resulted from that source of power or energy. Every fragmentary energy or power has been personified into different living beings so, man is the best media of all fragmentary energies or powers. In this respect, a question may occur to mind that men are nothing but a reflected fragmentary particle of that power or energy, so people are too young in the scheme of vastness to find out its true mystery. As a result, one who contains the boundless energy or power called God is incomparable with both the animate and inanimate in this world. He is the superior to all. In wider sense, love is in the name of God or in the incarnation of God existing in every heart. Directly or indirectly, and consciously or subconsciously every man (even all living beings) is anxious for love. And both the world and life are full of love without which men can't move or pass a single moment in life.

And, every man is anxiously yearning after love, and man is a guest at the door of love under influence of gross knowledge, reasoning knowledge and subtle knowledge. According to the steps of knowledge, love becomes deeper from deep, and deepest from deeper, since then the idea of God becomes deep and profound amid the thought of love. Hence both love and God must be coincided with each other in life in this world.

I earnestly request you to yield to love through loving. You enhance and awaken the latent organs of perception and try your best to charm them with tune of love. You throw your two thirsty looks into the looks of your beloved, and strive to find out the meaning of her looks having judged by your mind!

Thus you start your everlasting journey through the judgment of your every organ of your corporeal body having come in contact with love. You see that your prolonged journey with your beloved (even any close one) will beget a realization regarding your life & world, where "God is nothing but a ladder of energy of consciousness with the help of which you may easily approach the lofty destination of your life. So I pray with my folded hands to Almighty to cast His auspicious blessing upon you; you should keep always opening the door of your heart to welcome your oldest friend and unasked guest, love'. Let love enter into your desert life. Let your life flourish with sweet buds and flowers. You look up and look forward to with the earnest eyes God must descend on your earthen floor of life; because you are still endowed with His fragmentary energy; you are His real friend. We are all beggars at the door of consciousness. If not, we would become the omniscient. In this respect, devotion is the best attraction to get love in every turn of your aggravated life. So devotion begets a profound attraction, which makes a bridge of love between two hearts regarding relation. Every best devotee is regarded as the best lover or the beloved. Being a human whether you believe in existence of God or not, it is not my question; but being a man you must respond to the hidden call of your consciousness. You can never violate this subtle and sublime attraction betwixt your corporeal body and spiritual mind (i.e. or soul). Such attraction is nothing but love, and this love is nothing but a sublime expression of God who has kept this subtle idea between this 'you' and yours you (i.e. real essence). So love is so sweet, because such separation gives birth to a lot of mysteries. Regarding love, separation sweetens every moment to think of this life more sweetly and beautifully. God seems to be the creator of this vast creation. And love itself embodies life in the light of consciousness being guided by the inner knowledge of the eleven organs including mind, for life is tasted so sweet in the presence of love. Whoever you may be, you never deny this true 'essence', which expresses you. Without it you are non-existent. If you have capacity you may go to the very beginning of this 'essence' along with the path of conscious knowledge on the basis of the mystery of the transmigration of the soul, for every life is endowed with a 'spirited essence'. Where 'spirituality' is its main recognition, there it comes in contact with life. Hence this life is spiritual. And a feeling of love becomes more and more deep to realize its occult, and since then man gets an immense joy. As a man feels a world of pleasure & gratitude reaching his expected destination in the mundane thought, a man gets a boundless enjoyment whenever he reaches his prolonged expectation amid a long journey on the basis of the widest sense. Thus man can conquer the true love having enhanced and realized his own essence. That time both love and God seem to be the same though they seem different entities externally. Love makes two hearts one. As a result, the power or the energy of love is superior to all. No mundane power or energy or force can prevent it from going ahead of struggling any critical situation. So, whenever any heart possesses love, it seems to be the boldest and bravest to violate any worldly conditions and barriers in the way of the truth. So, as God is endowed with the unlimited characteristics and qualities of supreme power, love is also crowned with endless sublime characteristics. Love and God are substitute for each other. Such type of qualities and characteristics must appear gradually in you when your will relies on love. So, thought of god rests on a true belief of one's essence that imparts a true relief to one's disquiet life. True consciousness begets true inspiration, resulting from "love", which stands for god.

FIFTEENTH CHAPTER

WHEN LOVE IS JUDGED IN LIGHT OF LOVE

Love teaches how to be right

Being a silent teacher,

Like a justice it judges life

By its miracle power.

The thousand of writers, poets, authors, philosophers, and the men of letters of different categories have placed their distinguished and pedantic and heart rendering opinions relating to love. I am very much inferior to them to make any comment on it. Yet I intend to touch a little upon this expected matter because it seems to be my subject matter.

I have no wish to discuss it elaborately. I only want to give an emphasis on it in order to elucidate clearly for getting its purport. We all know that love is as old as the world itself. It is the primal source and inspiration of this beautiful creation. After all, love is above all. Without love no creation is possible on this earth. Having kept in mind of its proper application you have to go ahead in respect of your life. Please wait a while my readers, let me state it in its way. I am thinking of explicating it (i.e. love) on the basis of general view, which seems to be universal and scientific outlook also. I do mind that real love never comes into effect amid pre-understanding and foreseeing. What we mean by true love comes into being spontaneously without pre-knowing, pre-understanding, foreseeing and preplanning. Do mind, spontaneity is the life of love. Love begets spontaneity. Both love and spontaneity are substitute for each other. So it is evident that real love occurs in a true spontaneous way under the impact of inherent unseen force of intuition of life. Man is a wonderful creation in this wonderful world. So, owing to knowledge he is regarded as the best of all creations in this vast world. For this reason man has acquired the best capacity to adopt himself to this creation by dint of his unseen force and the unspoken thirst of his hidden heart.

It can be said in the light of scientific outlook that real love also follows characteristic of the Darwin's Law of Natural Selection. Where is no spontaneity, there is no love. That love comes in human life through preplanning, understanding and foreseeing is not considered a real love. Though from the outside it seems to be love but it has no value in the essence of love. Mind is very much curious, mysterious and singular, so it goes on thinking of and discerning spontaneously with. No force can hinder it from pondering over and going ahead of facing any unknown mysterious and the occult. Besides, in accordance with religious view love is a heavenly bliss. It is a ray of heavenly benediction. Mind (i.e. heart) is the proper abode of love. As mind can't be seen, love is also unseen. It is only felt and perceived intuitively. It can be discerned with mind and heart.

So it can be pointed out that man can't live without oxygen, which can't be seen. It seems to be unseen matter or power, but it pervades everywhere. Like that man feels uneasy in lack of love-like oxygen. Though this is unseen and invisible thing, its presence is very essential and indispensable in mind. When mind is void of love-like oxygen, it turns into a depressed toy. In spite of moving he loses his balance of mental power resulting from love. Love begets an invisible power and inner energy of mind. And love provides a man with will power, inspiration and true balance of standing and thinking. Love may come of several sources. It may deduce from both your individual and family life, but always you have to be conscious because mind is the main container of love. So from the very beginning, you should take care of your mind, container of love. For the matter of love, first and foremost you should be attentive to make your mind acceptable and suitable for partaking of love. If mind is not able to gather an immense power to accept love, it will not be possible for any one in his personal life to have any panoramic outlook regarding anything to enhance the dormant faculties of humanity, individuality as well as sanctity for adopting himself to this society. To make energetic the feeble mind and the cells of mind love is indispensable, because they (i.e. cells of mind) lose their power of thinking of a new subject matter indulged in pondering over the false and the shame like filtrations. I desire to say a few words as to love. Love is an unseen power that influenced the inner world of mind, and this mind acts like radar to guide this life. Such unseen power can be only felt. Love is a beautiful belief on which a man can rely and flourish his humane characteristics and faculties. It is such a belief that leads a life smoothly to its ultimatum. It is construed in another way that love is nothing but a sacred expression of hidden heart, for without heart love cannot be made to speak out its unspoken words. So, heart's expression is the best expression of love. It is the best media and abode of love. It is sure that love can't be confined to a few definitions or words. It is just like water, as water takes the shape of any container in which it is put. So, you should always dwell upon it that mind is just like a container. Whole matter rests on the capacity of mind. If your mind is a large container you can contain plentiful love like holy water, and with which you will be able to bathe, and quench your thirst when you wish. In order to confer over it, I could not stop opening my heart without pointing out some relevant matters about love. I utmost try to discuss love in a logical way on the basis of philosophy, for life and love can't be comprehended minutely and conspicuously without delving into the depth of philosophy. In this case I am trying my best to elucidate love. My readers, please you think whether it is acceptable or not. Love is an aggregate of life (Jibana), world (Jagata) and Philosophy (Darshana). So, I do mind nothing is out of love.

However little, a man grasps the essence of love, I do mind that'll be enough for a life to shaken all type of frustration, suffering and agony associated with mind. Love is totally a matter of heart. No external thing can't be mixed with it. If love seems to be an ocean, every life seems to be a river murmuring for joining with the ocean. That the river has no tide and web cannot follow spontaneously in course of time. Such river will turn into a standstill river, and then it is not called a river. River means following, wavy, speedy and murmuring. I expect all of my friends to take this point into your mind for realizing at every step of your life. Without 'love' life is just like stagnant water, which only gives birth to a lot of germs. Without diversity life is void of essence. So everybody should keep in mind that love begets exhilarated diversity in life. It leads a life to the goal of universality through simplifying worldly adversity.

Here is my question—if you look around and try to ponder deeply, such thought may touch the bottom of your heart. In all cases of life, can we pass a single step instead of love? In the presence of love like light all hearts seem cheerful. How is there possible to fall the darkness of confliction, agony and frustration? Why is the life loaded with vanity, disparity and pride? Why is life pining and waning for unhappiness, sorrow and frustration? Why is man not able to trust to each other? Why? Without love we can't pass a moment. Have we tried to realize that love? Are we really in our essence? Are we truly applying love in our life? I invoke and welcome all classes of people irrespective of caste and creed to revolutionize love in every sphere of their life to embrace a happy life. So its light prevails all over the world.

SIXTEENTH CHAPTER

WHAT IS LOVE PILL?

What love carries is all charming.

Nothing is bitter in its meaning

As SHIVA sucks all venom

And makes life sweet and calm

I am desirous of telling a few words to my readers before thrashing out love pill. I have discovered this love pill keeping an eye on this decadent society to which we all are still belonging. It is sure that this family, society and state, even the whole of the world never be existed in its proper name without the people. Thus you think so it will be clear that from individual to family, family to society, society to a state, from a state to a nation, even the whole of the universe. In this respect, we all know that without population a family, a society, even a nation can't be thought manifestly and conspicuously regarding the existence. If you are asked where you are still standing concerning your personal and family life in this society; what would you think of this expected matter? Perhaps, some question may appeal to you. are such family and society suitable for living a peaceful life? Like you, if others can be requested to tell the answer they will give answer almost the same! How can a society or a family itself destroy? How it is possible! Only we are going to blame the family or the society, but we are not realizing that such family and society never comes into being by itself. Always we should think that we have given the shape of a family, society, state and so on. And we are positively responsible for the destroying of this beautiful, dreamy family and society which are the dream land of our childhood, and the first place for learning of A, B, C and abode like Brindabana of the youth and grave of the last stage of our life. Truly speaking, people are too contracted the illness of immortality, perversity and inhumanity to think of a secure family and society. So I concern that this love-pill will be apposite for curing people of such fatal germs and will make people think of stratagem for building up a new society where people be able to live a peaceful life. The germ of this decadence has crept into the core of heart from individual life to the social life; even it spreads all over the world.

If it is true; how should we eradicate such germ of destruction? Are you anxious about this dilemma? Be patient, and listen to what my pen desires to tell you! Really if you long for a happy and peaceful life, you ought to prevent your family and society from extirpating, First and foremost you must be aware of yourself. you have to take a broad outlook regarding your 'personal life'; you should first prevent your 'personal life' from receiving in the question of 'the value of in humanity'. you should learn a lesson how to seek after a happy, peaceful and beautiful life. So you will be able to hug a happy or peaceful life driving away all the destructive germs from you. Since then you must be able to finding out a lot of clues to save your family and society from ruining. We are also representatives of the same decadent society. We all are also victims of this society and carrying on the germ of this decadent society. A lot of colourful dreams of my two destitute eyes have turned into surge of warm tear. My friend! I desire to acquaint you with a strange 'thing'—called 'love pill'. Perhaps, it may be regarded as a 'panacea'. Hope it may be a remedy for your entire mental malady if you dream of a happy life, peaceful family and felicitated society. Remembering it, this 'love-pill' must fulfill your dream.If you hanker after becoming a man of sound mind, you must be a giant for taking this love-pill regularly. By constant taking this love-pill you must come round from your all-chronic mental discase. Once you are habituated to this love pill, so no germ can touch you. besides, in course of time you will be able to increase energetic power for fighting against the harmful germs, which hinder your humane, beautiful and true qualities/ characteristics from flourishing spontaneously. When this 'love-pill' will be your friend' it must cure your all sort of uneasiness, frustration and despair, and also headache as to this mundane burden. It must succour you to make a proper man keeping pace with the advanced world of humanity. Under the influence of this love-pill the activities of your both perceptive and active organs will be activated and energetic. Even the nerve of every organ will be introvert in the question of humanity.

SANKAR SARKAR

I have discovered this love-pill amid a lot of experiences. And you will be also successful in many a case, specially, those who will take this love-pill they must get an immense result both in their individual and family life. And its effect is far-off important. Day-after-day man strangles his belief in others. They are drawing themselves back from the state of true belief. We are also on forgetting the bondage of blood relation. Why? Have you thought of its dark aspect of your life? Our life is the most wonderful gift. But we are too sophisticated and self conceited to appreciate such wonderful gift. Please, my friends, approach towards my thought, and let your mind think of and take a wide outlook in respect of the state your of mind. It is not possible for us to think of curing our family and society from destruction until we are able to cure our own ailments. So, you don't fritter away time in vain. You have to take care of your own 'personal life' to build it up fettle and active. And you need to augment your resistant power for confronting the fatal germ of inhumanity that eats into the essence of life. So, to improve this power you must be accustomed yourself to love-pill. Are you really happy? Are you getting your expected peace from your close-ones for whom you trudging hard? Perhaps, you have swallowed a handful of assorted 'pills' for your different ailments. Thus you have had a lot of bitter experiences in taking sundry 'pills'. And a deep antipathy is still lingering in your mind to any 'pill' as a remedy for your malady. but your laziness in every step of your life since the dawn of your flourishing of knowledge in the question of humanity begets fatal malady that is disheartening you gradually.

I don't know whether my writing will get a refuge in the corner of your mind or you will accept me as your friend or your well-wisher. After all, I do not have a little idea of your desire, because whole matter rests on your personal disposition and intention. Sometimes I hesitate whether I insist on you taking this matter! I have no wish to kill your precious time. It is my friendly requests all of you to apply it in your bitter life. I hope your various problems regarding your life may come to a close. You may get a ray of hope for living a peaceful life freed from all tensions in life. There are assorted types of tensions relating to your mind, such tension gives birth to a dozen of ailments in course of life. Day-after-day it shatters both mental and physical strength. It makes man detached from doing any inspired and enthusiastic work in life. Are you really yearning after a tension free life? If true, you take this love-pill as your companion. I think love-pill will be your only friend, which could recover you from all your tensions at every step of your life. I expect you a tension-free life. You must find after a while how I shall discuss its productive compositions, which are very much important and essential to your life. Its every composition plays a significant role to activate and renovate every inactive and sunken nerve of your body including mind. You must keep in mind that—its proper application imparts you a true realization for a happy life. Its every composition also causes a wide activity in your life. Perhaps, you must have observed that—how all compositions have collectively become active as well as wide in their scopes. Wait a little, my friends! I want to explicate this love-pill before discussing its compositions and far-reaching activity.I hope that you may get a new direction of your life to make your life more smooth and simple and accessible. In spite of this love-pill within the reach of your hand why you are not taking. Why you are wandering as a forlorn. So it is a matter of surprise that we all are aspirants for a happy and peaceful life, but for what things we are anxious we have not proper knowledge of the essence of these things, for our thought is not able to dive into the very heart of any subject matter. we all are always redundant and superfluous as to thinking of and giving any importance to any significant matter.

Concerning the expected matter, the present society is insecure for living with a peaceful mind. people are contracted the illness of immortality, perversity and inhumanity, which are deadlier than others. People are blindly blaming their family and society, but they don't think that they are the prime cause of it. Positively they are responsible their precarious life. After all our family and society also feel the want of the cured life. It is sure that a cured as well as sound mind begets a sound stratagem respecting the structure of a new family and society. So, I mind that love—pill will be more proper selection or medicine for killing such incurable germs than the handmade medicine.

SEVENTEENTH CHAPTER

HISTORY OF LOVE PILL

Let life have love perpetually,

Let life realize love intently

To make this life honey

In the prolonged journey

Life is really sweet, not bitter

If love does not renounce it ever

In this chapter I am thinking of speaking of the history of love-pill how I had discovered it. I find it difficult how I shall start this story to you. Though it is not a long story, its history of discovery, perhaps, will be enough touching and attractive. With a mindful of hope I am approaching towards you to open my shut door of heart. I don't know what little I shall be able to quench your thirsty heart. My readers! At every step of my thought of any stern aspect you are my encouragement, hope and pleasure for my poor mind. I have been thinking of going to Burdwan for a few days for an urgent piece of business; but for want of time it was not possible for me to go to Burdwan. At last I firmly decided to pay a visit to Burdwan and I did so. Whenever I made up my mind to go to somewhere for any piece of necessary work, I would face various types of obstacles; such incidents are not new matter in my life. So, it is a peculiar characteristic of my character to accustom myself to such tiny or petty disturbance. However sweeter life becomes while going ahead it encounters ordeals. When I faced various problems to do solve a piece of an important business in my life, yet I thought that my labour has not been in vain. The more life faces impediments, the more it will be hopeful. Such thought of life reminds the thought of death so life seems to be more romantic and optimistic; and then philosophy comes into being on the basis of entity. Such thought often puzzled me, but I got lots of pleasure. That work is accomplished through struggle must bring a good luck. Having done such work I felt much delight within myself. Perhaps, such word will not be suitable for you. But I am always aspirant for such a joy. However, such circumstances procrastinate me to tell you for what I have held my pen.

It was about the end of May. I got up early in the morning and finished my all-necessary duties in a haste manner. Because I have to catch a 9 O'clock train from Dum Dum Station, which is about the distance of twenty five kilometers from my residence, so I had to start for Dum Dum at 8.15 a.m. from my home, and I did so. However, I got Dum Dum junction before 10 minutes of the arrival of Burdwan Local Train. By this time I bought my ticket for my destination. The train got into station on scheduled time. I entrained quickly and got a seat beside the window on the left side of the train. The train was not so crowded. Most passengers of the compartment in to which I got are office-goers; and they were looking fresh. I was watching the natural scenery through the window; such natural deep attraction makes me forget all petty and prosaic attraction for this earthy life. its sacred and tranquil beauties were providing the thought of reality of this vastness with my mind; though it is for a while, yet it seemed the thickest attachment that anchored into the very depth of my heart since a long before. So, being absorbed in the thought of the unuttered words of nature I was endeavouring to go back to the lost trace of intimacy had been left in my poor heart. Such thought took me many a mile back to make a relation with the present. It seems that I was then still on the threshold of endless tranquility.

When I woke up from the state of trance, I found myself among many new faces with which my two eyes have not been acquainted before a few minutes. I did not understand when the train has already left three stations behind. A middle-aged couple had filled two vacant seats in front of me. They seemed they were still belonging to the gentry; but the gentleman looked ill. I think he was suffering from any uneasiness. After a while it was conspicuous that he had a bad headache with fever, because his two eyes' colour was reddish, generally it occurred due to augmenting in temperature of body. However, I was looking around in that compartment, all of a sudden a lovely maid of about nineteen or twenty was caught in my sight. She was just sitting opposite to my seat beside a window. She looked very nice. It seemed that her beauty and romantic countenance triumphed over the vanity of the fair sex of this compartment. Truly speaking, my two eyes were engrossed in partaking of the sweet nectar of the beauty of this wonderful creation. I thanked much of its creator. I thought my two eyes got quenched thirst. It seemed that she was a dripping new-bloomed flower from the tree of beauty of heaven. I told within myself, how God's creation sweet may be! She was clad in white colour cloth with fabric handwork, and simple designed border. After all her every inch of body was replete with beauty. It is sure that God's gift can be realized and displayed beautifully through simplicity. So simplicity is the essence of reality of beauty. But, she was looking grim and sad. why? What was she seeking for? It is like a pace of cloud wandering in the moonlight night. What little I discerned her was suffering from some unknown, unuttered and unspoken sorrow. She was just like a drenched lily in the water of sadness. I almost stared at her for a few minutes steadily. I could not grasp what unseen attraction was gradually overwhelming me. Whoever she may be—it was not a great question to me! She was a great and fantastic media of beauty, which is vested with unseen Supreme Power! So I felt also sorry for her sad plight; She was steadily sitting and gazing at something out of the window. She was fully unaware of any incident about her. There was not a single man whose glance did not fall upon her. However, I tried to make understand my mind to cope up with such situation. I turned my eyes then to the passengers of my front seats. I felt that the middle aged gentle man was suffering much from high fever and a bad headache. My heart was writhing with his agony! But I had nothing to do but observing. After a while, I drew the attention of the gentle lady, wife of this gentleman, and I said "kindly you get his head on your shoulder, aunty! He is feeling much pain! She glanced at me with smiling and held hastily his head, and she told her husband to put his head on her shoulder. The gentle man slowly put his head on her shoulder. She touched his forehead and whispered within herself, how temperature it is! In twinkling of an eye she took out a water pot and a package of medicine from her beautiful-decorated bag. She tore away the package of medicine and took out also a single pill quickly and gave it to and requested him to swallow this pill with a little water. The gentle man took the pill with his weak hand from her and swilled it with a little water of the pot. At that time a man asked where you would go. The gentle woman answered that they would go to Burdwan. again the speaker asked, where? Getting Burdwan? The speaker, also, answered in accordance with her, that he must help them; he would also go there. Having heard his word the woman got an assurance. My two eyes now and then were watching that girl who was still sitting with a heavy-heart. It seems she was just like a depressed-toy. Frustration, despondency and despair have obsessed her. As if she was groping something in the darkness of the hopelessness! So she looked weaker than that of the gentleman who was attacked with fever. She was nothing but a withered flower to me. In course of time it was seen that within fifteen minutes the gentleman got perspired and felt a little relief. Pill gave him enough relief from both temperature and headache! Suddenly my glance fell on the package with which the pill was coated. This pill was 'Parasitamol' which was an antibiotic against fever, headache& pain. Even its compositions had also been printed on this coated paper. I was trying to read carefully the name of its compositions, at that time the train was slowly getting at the station. Then that bereaved girl was peeping through the window and her two thirsty and wistful eyes were looking for someone. As soon as the train touched at the Station, a boy of medium height in white complexion about twenty-two or twenty-four, was approaching towards her having caught her sight from a distance with busy foot-step; and he handed over an envelope like folded paper, small in size, to her through the window. The girl took it earnestly and quickly from that boy. As the train was in motion, the boy told her loudly by name 'Showly'—'don't think; he is yours. You'll wait there till 5 p.m. No sooner had she heard such words from that boy than her tired eyes got flashed with delighted-tear. In a trice she awoke from the state of her despondency. a ray of hope and pleasure fell upon her face. She opened that envelop with her lovely and magical white fingers. on this envelope a love-sign was inscribed beautifully. She was reading this letter with rapt attention, the more she was feeling romance & thrilling. Within one or two minutes she came round from her ailments which made her a weak and hopeless like a withered flower before a few minutes. These two incidents occurred in front of me. What I had witnessed myself. One patient was attracted with high fever accompanied with a bad headache, so he looked weak physically on the one hand; on the other hand the another patient (i.e. girl) looked more weak and depressed than that of the gentleman, which influence left a deep impression on her mind, and it also affected her body. Two incidents occurred subsequently under my nose. such two incidents impressed upon and crept into my mind.

It is a wonderful matter that a few words activated as an elixir of life, which brought back a new hope and dream to her depressed and hopeless life under the impact of its unseen and hidden action. The girl was spirited and energetic. In a trice she got drenched with the stream of pleasure. How was it possible? What powerful those words were? Even it seems that those words inscribed on the piece of paper were hundred times stronger than that of medicine, which relieved the gentleman's illness. After two stations I saw that girl getting down from train with a flash of smile on her lip. But she left a hint upon my curious mind. I gave her a lot of thanks within myself. Since then my mind started its prolonged journey along with this trace of hint that had been left by the girl. I had to pass many a day in order to finding out the real nuance and subtle comparison, and even the similarity on the basis of the coated pill (i.e. as an example 'Parasitamal') and a love letter covered with a love sign envelope just like a package of a coated medicine.In course of time, an idea occurred to me. Like the compositions of a distinctive medicine, 'love' has also specific compositions; and every composition has a fixed role of activity just like a medicine. If it is true, why it will not be possible in respect of love. If 'love' may be taken for a 'pill', and if its name is given 'love-pill'-How it is! Such thought made me thrilling. My heart was overwhelmed with unuttered joy and two eyes got melted into pleasant tears instantly. Again and again I said to myself that this 'love-pill' will be an excellent medicine, even it will not be a little wrong if it is called 'Panacea' that may be a remedy for all ailments and maladies. I don't know whether I have enabled to open my heart to you or not; or whether my discussion is appropriate for appreciating your precious time or not.

Thus a few days had been passed. But my thought did not come to a close. It had rather got proliferated day-after-day. Two incidents of that day left a profound impression upon my mind. Such interesting matter of incidents made me think seriously. Since then I was on feeling a smell of invention that was still hovering about me. One incident is a coated pill (i.e. a medicine named 'Parasitamol'), which relieved that gentle man's suffering, and the second incident is a piece of folding envelope like white paper on which a love sign was drawn. it seems to be also a coated pill that brought back the life force to that broken-hearted girl. As that coated pill (i.e. parasitamol) has a distinctive 'power', because every 'Pill' consists of some specific elements or compositions. It is evident that each element or composition has a distinctive active role separately. But the power of coated pill (i.e. suppose Parasitamol) seems to be inferior to the power of coated pill which had been swallowed by that broken-hearted girl with the water of feeling: Here is a point of interesting that coated-pill (i.e. Parasitamal) is only appropriate and suitable for relieving the physical suffering and agony for a short period of time; but love sign coated-pill seemed more powerful because it relieved the girl both of her physical & mental suffering & agony. Because any malady which originates from the matter of mental aspect, which also affects much physical side of a man & it leaves a deadly affect over life; in this respect, its activity is prolonged and deep. Perhaps, my all-wise readers must conjecture my invention. So, on the basis of these two incidents I had come into a fixed decision that like coated-pill (i.e. Parasitamal), the love-sign coated-pill is more powerful medicine; though both applications are contrary to each other. However, thus I discovered my love-pill, here love-sign coated-pill whose name was given 'love-pill. I think it is also composed of a few distinctive elements or compositions whose roles of activity are more powerful and energetic than those of any other medicine.

Truly speaking, both the life and the world are still getting immersed into the ditch of destruction, and endless frustration. So, if you want to protect your family & society from this utter destruction; at first you must try to save yourself from any incurable germ of malady of frustration. Under the circumstances, this love-pill will be only remedy for the germ of incurable malady, which eats into the essence of the life. Always one should remember that the germ of inhumanity is very much harmful to one's life. And from this germ many an incurable malady gets germinated in course of time It becomes a main cause of all frustration and destruction. If truly you long for a happy life or family and a society, firstly you have to be a happy man, and you must be a man of a fresh mind. the power of thought of your mind must be strong and proper, true & sacred, and durable &prolonged, then no frustration and despair can touch your life. In order to widen and strengthen one's mental power, one must take love-pill to flourish all one's latent human-faculties. One must keep in mind that only love-pill is the remedy for fighting against the germs of all frustrations, and inhumanity. By its proper application a man can enjoy a true happy life. Its unseen far-off reaction sweetens life. If you think deeply, you must grasp that we are all almost the patients of this love-pill. I must discuss its effect and role in life relating to its every composition in the next chapter.

EIGHTEENTH CHAPTER

COMPOSITIONS OF LOVE-PILL

Before discussing the compositions of Love-pill I wish to touch a little upon the matter of 'love' once for all in the 'A new philosophical classic: Theory of Love'. though in the previous chapter I have conferred over many a topic regarding 'love', yet it seems to be unveiled somewhat about 'love' without pointing out a single aspect in respect of the 'abode' of love. In the inner world 'love' is a great invisible shelter for 'mind' regarding life, which just like an axis around which other organs of this body revolve on. So, you build a house to save your mortal body from all precarious conditions of the outside ambience. Like it, to keep your 'mind' in the state of tranquility, firstly you have to build up the 'abode of love' that only can save you from disquiet state. In order to construct the abode of love-faithfulness, uprightness, renunciation and self-dedication are very much indispensable for building up it for these four elements act like the four pillars for the 'abode of love'. If you want to sweeten your life, you should prevent yourself from inquietude, anxiety, disturbance and frustration, which are your great nuisance for annoying your quiet mind. So you must endeavour to erect this abode of love by dint of these four pillars without which such 'abode of love' is not possible. So, if you once build it up, you will truly be a happy man, because nothing could exterminate this abode. Since then your shelter will be best one for pleasure. But we are so aberrant and emotional for adorning up the adobe of love that we forget the proper necessaries and procedures to structure it.Its span is not prolonged longevity, and is not everlasting. Here it is obvious that we build up our 'abode of love' in an emotional and unconscious trance, besides we explain it in the wrong way and also by a wrong name. So, we can't have love in spite of constructing the 'abode of love' in life. Because we forget the true elements to utilize in the time of building up this abode amid proper way, so we suffer from various detrimental ups and downs in course of our long travelling along with the uneven path of life. I request all of you to cogitate over this matter at least once before entering this abode in life. This abode is better and more necessary than the shelter of the outside. I don't know what little I am able to open my heart to you through my ignorant pen that is eagerly looking forward to your warm contact in this dam and sordid atmosphere of inhumanity.

Having given the above discussion I intend to go back to the expected point on which this chapter has been selected. I want to speak of the compositions of the Love-pill about which two chapters have been treated previously concerning love-pill and 'History of love pill'. I hope you might have got an edge of conjecture regarding love-pill going through the preceding discussion. Now let me touch upon it. Whoever you may be! Whatever your profession may be! What class of people do you belong to? What of that? It is not my question! Here is my question that you are a man; and you are getting embroiled yourself in to several imbroglios in life. Suffering from various troublesome your mind is having debilitated day-after-day. As a result, in spite of living in the family or in a society you find it very hard to cope with the others, even with your close ones with whom you are spending most of time in your daily life. Besides you find yourself a sequestered one from them.

Have you thought of why you are not able to keep pace with the others? Why are you not apposite to succour yourself in such precarious state? Your mind has become so enervated to think of any constructive aspect inconformity with life. In many previous chapters I have spoken of 'mind' that is a central point for judging any essential aspect whether it is accessible or not by the other ten organs; specially five organs of perception. In order to revamp the mind and guide your life smoothly to the proper path you need love-pill. I do mind it will be only remedy for fighting against all types of inhuman germs, which beget a lot of malady, to suck the life-blood up and reduce a life to the skeleton on asking the essence of life. On account of undergoing such malady man is compelled to forget all human characteristics. such prolonged suffering has made man perverted. it seems his life is deviated from the natural or normal state. If it is observed, it will be obvious that almost ninety-nine percent people in every family or society all over the world are victims of such perversion, which is devoid of human manners. For this reason, people in every family or society all over the world are victims of such perversity. So every family, society and state face this unending and uncertain perversity. As a result people are smouldering for want of security; even a man is insulted and humiliated by another man. being a man he can't expect a little security, certainty, belief and assurance to others relating to the question of humanity. How is it possible for a man to live in a peace? How will he make his family or society a secure place for living a happy life? With which medicine could you cure yourself or your family of such perverted diseases? My friend! Trusting me you may stretch out your altruistic hand to take this medicine which I am eagerly offering to you and hope this medicine will be enough and suitable for healing all your maladies.

To get the full-fledged taste of this beautiful life at first you have to surmount all types of perverted ailments, which are responsible for disquiet, anxiety and frustration in life. In this respect, you are requested to take this love-pill to alleviate these fatal maladies so that you may get back the quiet state of your mind. To lessen or assuage the agony of your suffering you may take this medicine whenever you wish. Because it is a gratis piece of pill which can usher plenty of relief in your agonized life instantly and its prolonged reaction must bring sustained peace throughout your life.

If you yearn after a happy life, this 'pill' will be substitute for that. And it will augment all kinds of good characteristics for resistant power both in your body and mind to defeat all evil symptoms. You may believe in the activity of this 'pill' to bring down all tensions relating to your restless life. Four best symptoms will be visible through the using of this "love-pill". They will display vital roles for bringing a ray of hope in life. It also revamps both your body and mind in full swing. So, the more you will prolong such symptoms, the more you will feel exhilaration in your every walk of life having forgot exhaustion with regard to your languorous body and mind. It also gives birth to a new dream in your mind to embrace a peaceful life in your stringent journey. After all the applied love-pill begets a lot of bright symptoms that seem to be presage of a pleasant life. By dint of it you must feel a change in your mind, and its inward flow will please you. And such symptoms provide you with self-confidence, which makes you, believe in others. Such symptoms are substitute for the true symptoms of humanity.

Truly speaking, the whole of our body is full of scars left by the prolonged malady of inhumanity. Without proper treatment its condition becomes worse. Like a contagious disease it pervades its incurable germs from which even no man is able to save himself. Wherever you look, there is pale and hopeless face contracting such malady. If you want to feel a sound sensation for every moment about your body and mind in your daily life you should take love pill, which is undoubtedly without side effect. I have a good belief in its profound activity for ushering immense pleasure and happiness in your stern life having alleviated all agony of the sores both in your body and mind. So, you may think that the proper remedy is at your hand for your malady that pines and suffers you much. Undoubtedly it can be told that almost ninety percent people are victims of this peculiar malady for their utter indifference and callousness regarding their own reality of essence. As a result they are compelled to spend day after day in the midst of stoic. And its consequence is taking a gruesome shape in life. My friend! You never forget that you are still belonging to this group. And in course of time our languidness and carelessness may lead us to the jaw of death and to the hell. It is a matter of surprise that you are unconsciously contracting such malady, as a result you are too enervated to leave a long road behind and proceed facing all difficulties and sufferings on your way to any fixed destination in life. Such a matter renders you a hopeless. It begets disappointment, despondence, dejection, despair and frustration. If you intend to have a happy life, you must take this love-pill as remedy for curing yourself of these fatal symptoms.We are too modern to respond to the proper call of our own self. We are too sophisticated to respond to the true relation. now any relation has become repulsion that is nothing but musk or a false screen that is stronger than that of a thick-brick wall of a room. So the poverty of the morality in life is too dominated that it is very impossible for a true mind to survive.

In this respect, I request you don't let your entity burn with fire of perverted love. Please you never apply your love in the way of perversity. You have lost the power of thinking, so you are on misexplaining almost every vital matter, which instills the life-blood into you to fight against all obstacles throughout your sustained journey in your life. What remedy will be apposite for mitigating your unuttered agony and will give you a lasting relief? Come back my friend! Come back! Don't flirt away the precious time of your life. Don't let yourself immerse in the uncertain state. to resurrect your lost power and energy in your body and mind you should start taking this love-pill since now. You keep in mind that only love-pill is such a remedy which could impart the resuscitation to all your shattered organs. Then you will find that your all-obsessive organs including mind promptly resume their respective activities under the influence of love-pill. Like a hand-made 'pill' it has also a considerable number of compositions. Its each composition plays an important role in your body and mind. Though a hand-made pill alleviates your pain, but its span of longevity is not more. but love-pill has prolonged longevity. Having killed all disquiet manners and anxieties it may derive from any source. It is obvious that only love-pill can bring about comfort in your life, however little.And life is speedy regarding 'curiosity'; without 'curiosity' life is tasteless and insipid. So, if you want to judge your life, then it should be judged in the light of liveliness that is substitute for 'curiosity'.' Curiosity' never comes into being in life in absence of 'love'. Life, which is devoid of humanity, is bereft of true love that sustains 'curiosity' throughout life.

In order to sustain this 'curiosity' in every walk of life you have to uphold your inner spirit, which is enlightened by the purified power of love. But we are too steeped in the materials to assess the true matter of entity of life. we are still clinging tenaciously to the uncertainty, as a result, gradually we get shattered our spirit in a precious way. Despite knowing its dark consequence we are not conscious of improving our penury plight. Though it is easy for you to visit any wonderful place of this material world with the pursuit of wealth, but it is very much hard to paying a visit any evergreen and ever pleasant land of mind which seems more wonderful, even most wonderful land to keep on you cheerful and lively providing the feast of pabulum with your thirsty life. O my friend! Don't let your sacred spirit get dried up! You get love-pill and spirited yourself. This world is not for the weak is for the strong. So, you try to be strong both in body and mind relating to sanctity and humanity. You partake of beauty both of the world and life to appease yourself. I exhort you to have this love-pill for resurrecting the fresh spirit in life. I again request you to be in communion with love-pill. It must make you good feel in every turn of your work to forget all sorrows of life. You should believe in the activity of love-pill. I can assure you never get cheated and frustrated having this remedy for the purpose of curing your diseases that lead degree by degree you to the death. Only love-pill could make you inspire to face any difficulty and trouble, besides it can cure your deadly maladies of skepticism and dejection. You are revitalized under the healing balm of love-pill. And it will forge a tone link between two beautiful hearts. O, my friend! Let you essence engage in search for wealth of blithe spirit, not any wealth for materials health to hold any being only spellbound.

However little, "curiosity" is a sort of majesty of life, but love is a middling to sustain the equality between 'majesty' and 'life'. So, to keep on both 'curiosity' and 'majesty' pari passu with life the spirit of love must be par excellence. To bring about all activities in the normal manner regarding respective organs in life love-pill acts as a significant role as remedy. I hope it will be obvious to you through the analysis of its compositions as given below:

Compositions of love-pill:

I.   Beauty

II.   Sanctity

III.   Heartiness

IV.   Morality

V.   Sensitivity

VI.   Romance

VII.   Patience

VIII.   Passion

IX.   Compassion

X.   Emotion

XI.   Inspiration

XII.   Retention

XIII.   Separation

I don't know whether my writing will be useful to you or not. Yet I earnestly request you to ponder over the chapters of this book and exert it properly as far as possible in your life. I believe that it must awaken you from the state of disquiet. And life will veer to the happy & the rousing and sustaining of your own true 'essence' amidst keeping intact of sublimity and humanity in life. Thus it succours you to take a relish of life amid the brew of sorrows & pleasures throughout this prolonged journey.

If I stretch out my friendly hand towards you, my friends, would you really hold out your altruistic hand? Can I assure of your friendship? Tell me, would you not dishearten me? If it is, you never confine yourself in the pent of sordid thought. Please come out of the puzzled and open your heart to Live inwardly. You keep in mind that we all still belong to internality. and intensity of eternity begets more improbability, not certainty. So, you are properly responsible for the abrupt uncertainty in your every walk of life. For this you never blame others. but you may acclaim yourself for your own essence whose presence sustains you speedy and whose certainty gives birth to a lot of intensities of true 'love' towards your inward body! So, it is a matter of astonishment that despite blowing of the southern wind you are sitting away for the releasing of comfortable breath for your tiredness opening the northern window. In spite of waiting and breezing of spring at your door you are panting for unbearable oppression.

My friend, I am very glad, I am very delighted having read your pleasant face! Don't cast your face down in shame. Life is a mélange of sordid game, some time life is a game of fame where love lively teaches you how to love in the midst of the keen knowledge in every sphere of your life. So, to realize and enjoy every moment you need activate each organ of your body amid taking love-pill whose intensity converts you to the affinity & the beauty that convokes humanity and morality to usher in the true fame in the prolonged game of your life.

My friend, am I not killing your precious time of your life? Am I not becoming a reason for a tiresome to your quiet mind? Do I not become a gust to drip a newborn bud of your pleasure? Or am I not going to involve myself in deteriorating your sign of relief? Forgive me, if I become a cause for the breaking of the rhythm of your life-like lyric or a cause of irritation to sustain the inspiration in your life. If my writing provides a bit of relief to the grief of your restless life, let it dwell in your thought, however it is for a while.

NINETEENTH CHAPTER

TRUE BELIEF BEGETS TRUE RELIEF IN LIFE

Happiness and sorrow seem relative,

Till love becomes a goal of life.

Relief results from belief, while knowledge

Guides the whole of the life:

I am unveiling this chapter with a few words regarding love because 'belief' has been considered a petty commodity in the arena of modernity. Who will appreciate 'love lovingly in his life? So, I am afraid of placing the true goddess of 'love' before you, if you turn your face away in dissatisfaction or if you display your disgusting will towards her! Truly speaking, I am really disheartened, though I have held my pen in the very dear market of 'belief', because 'belief' is a kind of 'confidence', which assures you to go ahead of facing all predicaments. The poverty of belief begets inhumanity, when destiny gropes in the darkness of frustration;

life is then tired of with the flogging of disbelief; and consciousness then gets obsessed. Inspiration becomes consternation. Life is deserted for this you face a impede in every step of your life. Tell me, my friend! How is it possible to thrash out 'love'? Wherever you look there is a heart-rending cry. A sort of 'hollowness' and 'emptiness' are cropping up in mind. Uncanny feeling causes you panic in your every work. Why? Have you thought of why you are feeling such uneasiness and uncertainty always? Though your heart is bleeding for getting a little relief from the monotonous and puzzling heavy hours, yet it seems that 'relief' is far away beyond touching. Even, in spite of loving, you suffer disquiet, for day after day you are becoming hostile to 'belief'. you are throttling belief every moment. How will you yearn after 'relief' from your excruciating life? Always keep in mind that only true belief can usher relief in your life.

Because what you mean by 'love'—that is an embodiment of true 'peace' and 'pleasure'. but 'love'— stands on true 'belief'. Without 'belief' you never think of 'love'. Where 'love' is embodiment of the 'purified power' that exhilarates the inner world of your life, and it also induces the essence of life, so you are speedy and life like. It is evident that 'belief' is on the wane, so 'relief' is taking a prolonged leave from your life. For want of true belief you are on about out of breath of humanity. So 'love' seems to be a far-off thrush in the welkin of the imagination, and you are still in trance of love. Today you will be aghast that 'disbelief' causes the family & society overwhelmed with its poisonous breath. Even the whole of the nation is moldering for the keen frustration. My friend, I am no wishing to irritate and sadden you! I have intended to expose my agonized mind to you, but for lack of assurance of belief in your own veracity of essence I am reluctant or doubtful to shower my confidence upon you. Yet I request you to come back to your own kingdom of truthfulness where you first lost your 'confidence'! Your assurance and 'certainty' that had been endowed with you whenever you will get the traces and will be able to follow it along with the winding course of your life And such confidence makes you assure of yourself; and since then you will start feeling a sigh of 'relief' amidst 'belief'. On this point I assure you of this exigent matter that—the more your belief proliferates, the more 'relief' will accrue in your life. Where your 'belief' will grow more and more, there you will get relish of 'relief' more, because a strong belief begets deep love. Without 'belief' 'love' never unveils it to anyone. So 'love' augments in an equal proportion to the augment of 'belief'. Hence 'relief' comes into being from that life. You never forget that whenever your 'belief' in anyone grows more, then an invisible 'power' will grow in your mind, and your life feels a new enthusiasm that moves you forward confronting any dilemma in course of your restless life. Such spontaneous enthusiasm is nothing but the expression of love. Besides your 'belief' gets life centering any 'beauty' of 'anyone' and anything. Such 'beauty' is enchanted by itself and it holds you spellbound with its unseen power. So it is conspicuous that true 'belief' comes of 'true beauty' that is concomitant with 'love', and this 'love' begets true 'relief' in your exhausted, fatigued & monotonous life. Tell me, is relief possible in course of your life without 'belief'? If you want to have true 'relief' in your life, you must enhance and extend your belief in your close ones. Hence such 'belief' will usher in much 'relief' in you to enjoy life in an ecstatic way. So, you never let yourself at the disposal of density. Always keep in mind that— Destiny is the veracity of your duty. If such 'duty' is accomplished amid true 'belief', hence you may long for the taste of 'relief'. Every 'duty' is a shadow of 'true beauty' if it derives spontaneously from the inclination of your mind under the influence of consciousness. We are all victims of the sacred consciousness. So, 'relief' which is substitute for 'peace' 'pleasure' and 'happiness' have become now a very hardly possible thing in our life; and it is very hard to gain 'love' and seems to be a very far matter, though it (i.e. love) is still standing at the door of your life like an old guest. In conformity with this discussion, you should remember that-the more you acquire belief, the more you have love. Then 'relief' will descend spontaneously to your life. It is your first and foremost duty to attain 'belief' through your various relations regarding life. 'Belief' is the prime step in every walk of your life. So, always you have to remember that 'belief' seems to be the main basis of love. On the one hand, it gives birth to 'power'; on the other hand, this 'power' begets the 'belief' on which your life rests relating to several relations. In this respect, before 'love' you first build up your every movement of your life on the basis of true 'belief'. Until you can do this, you find it very difficult to love others and to get love from anyone. So, for want of 'belief' love becomes fruitfulness then. As a result, your life will be bereft of 'relief' Suppose with whom you are living day after day, but you can't win their mind and can't impress on them with your belief, even the others can't also make you believe, such restrained 'belief' never provides you with happy 'relief' in life. There you will find yourself confining in the island of 'disbelief'. As a result you are not able to relieve yourself from such isolated state of disbelief & you never quest after 'relief throughout your life. I am thinking of an exigent matter for a few days. I could not understand how I shall discover. But I don't know what thought and love at last unveiled the mystery of my mind. It is your unuttered love and friendship that have helped me to cogitate over this matter. Perhaps, your altruistic confidence has compelled me to expose my heart to you. If you deeply think so, it may be conspicuous to you, because whatever seems to be utter true and eternal such as, soul, mind, and life even this universe-the existence of these is never properly perceived without belief. Without keen and subtle belief and knowledge you are always ignorant of these both the animate and the inanimate. So, my friends you are not asked or not requested to believe in all. You have to believe in the being and things, which are useful to your life amid the judging by your knowledge and consciousness. Because without belief you never long for relief from the puzzling thought of any relation regarding this vast creation of which relation you are going to uphold yourself. that relation, however little, wants belief. Since then this relation offers you 'love' that only can make you happy and peaceful, and also make you a king of peace, otherwise you may be a forlorn in the world of peace and pleasure throughout your life. With regard to this expected point, you may be a rich man. You may have much wealth, but you are not happy. Because your belief is more in wealth than in with whom you are involved in deep relation. The more you deepen your relation with the inanimate thing, the more you lose your belief in the animate. So the 'relief' in your life will be reduced according to the proportion of your 'belief' in wealth or treasure. Then you never yearn after enough 'love', what little you should have expected to have. So, I request you to widen your scope of your 'belief' among your relative circles with which you spend most time of your daily life. You see then automatically the proportion of your 'love' will grow on, and will be then happy. Because, 'love' is a very rare thing so all think of and quest after it. You must keep in mind that unbelievable relation is like a weir of sand; where both 'relief' and 'love are futile. Thus you think so you will grasp that the mélange of belief, relation and relief begets 'love' in your life. This is inseparable so you are requested not to long for or quest after 'love' without seeking after belief in your expected ones. So, the more belief will be thicker regarding any relation, the more that relation will impart you deeper love. And since then you will get best relief from your belief relating to the angle of busy life. Perhaps the above discussion can be ended in this way that true belief is substitute for true love. What little belief you will acquire relating to any being, you will get this the same quantity of love in return from others. You will yearn after just little relief in your life in accordance with the degree of your love to others in respect of your belief. True belief begets true certainty regarding any relation that brings true love, which is responsible for relief.

TWENTIETH CHAPTER

LOVE IS TONIC

Love is an eternal hunger, life cherishes it till death:

Nothing can sate it so long it has breath

I am contemplating how I shall commence this chapter. The subject matter of this chapter enough puzzles me. An idea of frustration had been lingering in my mind. Whenever you will look around you must realize an emptiness of frustration is still cropping up and gradually engulfing both your individual and family life. Most people are impatient and anxious with the sting of such frustration and tension. Even ninety-nine percent people are getting themselves involved into this tension. Such tension is generally resulted from mental aspect. So it is a sort of chronic mental malady. It is sure that such type of despair is a positive drawback and hindrance in the way of progress of your life. A frustrated life always finds it difficult to get progress at every turn of life. So, once your mind suffers from such disorder that begets a dozen of frustrations. So it is not possible for you to get at the lofty destination having forsaken these. You think that your active life gets always entangled in a constant trouble, which gives birth to an endless frustration. When your life is weighed with a lot of frustrations, tensions and disappointment, you feel puzzle and confusion to do overcome it. For many a time to forget the tiredness and exhaustion of your agonized mind you indulge yourself in taking to tonic (i.e. wine), which refreshes and assuages your tired mind for a few minutes or hours. Its creation is not a long span. Even with this tonic you are never able to cure your chronic mental malady. Always you have to think that 'mind' is an internal organ, which is invisible and unseen; even not be touched by any mortal finger or limbs. Only it can be felt its presence with subtle feeling. However, a mind seems to be an abstract. So to alleviate the heaviness and tension of mind you have to take such type of tonic, which is made of the abstract elements. So, in this chapter I desire to acquaint you with a mysterious tonic, which will cure of your any mental tension and frustration. I do mind it will be unique for you. The name of that tonic is 'Love Tonic'. I can emphatically tell if once you can devote yourself to this tonic you must feel a tensionless joy for every moment. Because love is also abstract. It can't be placed on any specific general idea, and can be thought only on the basis of ignited idea, knowledge and philosophy. So, to mitigate any ailment (i.e. frustration, tension, despair etc.) associated with mind, that tonic must be derived from 'love'; because 'mind' itself is the expression of love, and love itself can express its weeny influence through mind. Because 'mind' may be blind of thinking and realizing addicted to the gross tonic this is devoid of love. So 'love tonic' is very essential for the resurrection of the real essence to a life.

So, in this chapter I endeavour my best to confer over love tonic. I don't know what little I'll be able to appease you with this, for you have tasted many world-renowned and famous tonics in the world. So my experience is much poor and inferior to your excellent experience. In this respect, I request once for all you to taste this love Tonic, you are also requested to compare this tonic (i.e. love Tonic) with handmade Tonic by your experience A matter of surprise that whenever the mental tiredness becomes more acute than physical tiredness, it becomes very detrimental to your life. Since then you will gradually lose your morale and courage even self-confidence to go ahead forsaking any critical and confused problem. And the activity of "Love Tonic" is deeper, sweeter and longer than the handmade tonic that shatters both your mental and physical strength day-by-day. So, I wish you to take "love tonic" and forget all despairs and uneasiness from your life, and enjoy a peaceful and tension free life. Physical fatigue can't debilitate you much as mental tiredness does. You are really tired and exhausted owing to heavy burden of your individual and worldly matters. In wider sense you are still on travelling and facing a lot of new problems constantly. Even your 'you' is downed with the weariness of long journey where is no 'starting' and ending on the ground of the thought of the transmigration of soul. However, I don't have a little wish to take you further into the thought of labyrinth.

So, I desire you to partake of love tonic and surmount the state of tiredness and despair in course of your hard life. You have to travel a long way. So always you have to remember that love tonic is your only energy tonic to forget the fatigue and laziness. And it always provides you with constant energy. Besides, its creative activity is a prolonged longevity. You should know that your corporeal body is its best container. Even you can produce this love tonic throughout your life. On the one hand, your corporeal body acts as a container of it, on the other hand, it also plays a vital role in the turn of production. It is a very singular and peculiar matter. I must manifest to you its singularity of production. Before discussing it I wish to talk over an interesting matter concerning the thought of external container of the hand-made tonic. As long as the container contains 'tonic' it has enough value and is considered a precious thing. And you will take then a fancy to this container, but whenever tonic is exhausted, this empty container is thrown away in the dustbin, and man forgets it forever. So, you should keep in mind your corporeal body is just like a 'container', which is replete with 'love tonic'. A 'tonic' is the essence of the container, called 'this corporeal body'. As long as your body is teemed with 'love tonic', hence it is so praiseworthy; and appreciated. If your corporeal body (means your life) is devoid of love-tonic, your life has no value. A life never becomes a meaningful and lively and energetic like handmade tonic (i.e. easily tonic). this love tonic is the essence of the corporeal body; in absence of this love tonic your life will be spiritless, lethargic and dull. Hence it is neglected and disregarded everywhere. Day-after-day your perceptive and active organs lose their proper activities. As a result you feel despair and despondency in your life to face sundry predicaments, because you are then too weak to think both of your own life and others. So, in order to surmount all types of dilemmas at every sphere of your struggling life you have to have love tonic to keep both you body and mind fresh and lively, energetic and active. Until you possess a sound health and courageousness in your mind you are not regarded as a true healthy man relating to your mental brevity. Your recognition and acquaintance exist as long as you are struggling for the true 'essence' of your life; and this true 'essence' is not thought fully in its state of spirit in absence of love tonic; which holds this 'true essence' spirited. So without it you are non-existent. In this respect, your ten organs of perception and action are always busy for collecting the expected necessary elements from the outside world accordingly their true scope of mysterious process for the purpose of the production of love tonic. These amassed elements can't be touched with the mortal finger and not be seen by naked (external) eyes. Because these seem abstract elements perceived with subtle idea and knowledge. Such elements are namely beauty, passion, romance, thrill, happiness, ugliness, mystery, feeling, goodness and so on. To make these collected elements that are necessary and useful for the productive purpose sorted by the inner organ called mind, which is leading the other organs, and these sorted elements are squeezed. This love tonic is prepared in your corporal body on the basis of the occult; where its density and quantity and quality are measured and judged by the measuring stick of knowledge under the proper guide of consciousness. After all, if you want to pass every moment in a good mood and rejoicing way, you must be accustomed yourself to love tonic. If you would like to enjoy the beauty of this vast beautiful world, at first you have to learn how to realize your 'you' by yourself. Since then such realization will provide you with proper inspiration to partake of the sweet-nectar of love for which you are always anxious for and overwhelmed. Let your mind avail itself of such opportunity. Don't abstain from having this love tonic to keep your corporeal body fresh and fit and pass the all day long through all energetic disposition and temperament. So the more you have love tonic, the more you have energy to go ahead. Are you weak? Are you a forlorn lover or beloved? Are you not able to cope with your struggling life? Are you an unrequited lover or beloved? Are you really anxious for love? Do you feel dizziness? Are you really not able to keep pace with the others? Please, you start instantly taking love tonic without squandering time. In the widest sense, as your corporeal body is the best container filled with love tonic to your beloved, as your beloved's corporeal body is also the best container full of love tonic to you, but you have to learn how to drink it. Mind that, love tonic has no side effects. It had rather influence the inner world of your life to improve your corporeal body to think of love and life relating to the world (because mind and ten organs are not out of this corporeal body).

So, I am going to close this chapter requesting you to quote these few words in your mind that-a drop of "love tonic" is so costly and rare in this world. Besides, it is too excellent to be available. So you must be aware and conscious of its quality; because a wrong quality of its potion may make your life miserable. If you look around, you must understand or realize how most people are suffering from mental disturbance with taking the wrong love potion, my friends! You are requested to take love tonic and be happy in your life in the proper way.

TWENTYONE CHAPTER

LOVE SPECTRUM

Love is like a powerful divine mirror,

That reflects both the near and the far

In order to make you understand clearly I have placed an example before you on the basis of a scientific matter, though I don't intend to give stringently emphasis upon this. I wish to exhibit this matter to have a conspicuous idea pertaining to both your body and love.

Gingerly you observe it will be pellucid to you that a prism is a good media to cause refraction of the solar spectrum by which it is explained that the sunlight consists of seven colourful rays though with our naked eyes we see that the sunlight seems to be white in colour. So, 'white' is not called any distinctive colour, because it is a compound. It is composed of seven colours. It has been tested with the help of a prism with its five surfaces.

In accordance with graphic figure I have a yen for comparing my expected subject. I hope you will get its proper idea about which I am intending to discuss. Here, human body has been compared to a 'prism' made of glass with five surfaces. Like it this body has also five surfaces. These five surfaces stand for five primary elements with which this gross body is made (i.e. soil, water, fire, space and air). Out of these the body is never imagined. So, whenever a ray of love like sun reflects through this gross-body, this love-light is refracted into seven colourful love-rays. It is quite impossible to grasp whether such colourful rays are present in 'love' or not. But its real character and nature get displayed amid human 'body' because human body is the best media to manifest the true nature of 'love'. In absence of "love" this human body cannot be realized properly in the question of the true acquaintance of 'man'. for a human being is considered as a real being with proper humane qualities. So, without humanity a man is not regarded as a true man. Respecting it, in the presence of these colourful rays of "love light' the darkness of inhumanity is gone off in life. Since then this body is internally turned into a proper thought of human body. These refracted seven colourful rays of love light are displayed through the activities of the life. And these colourful love rays are always being regulated and activated by the eleven organs of your body.

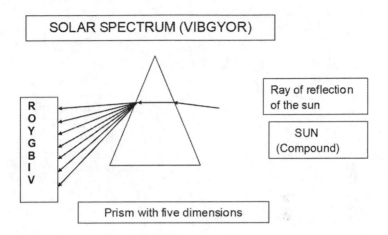

Five of them called sense organs and other five called the organs of action, and 'mind' is only internal organ. I hope you, of course, are able to get at its mystery of discerning. It is evident that love is "light" by which you can drive away the darkness of inhumanity from your life. Its force and power make you spirited to know the mystery of spirit of your essence. Your life expresses itself through different humane activities in presence of 'love'. This discussion must give you an extensible conception of 'love' that is omnipresent and omniscient. If you think this whole process in a subtle way, you must be glad of realizing its profundity.

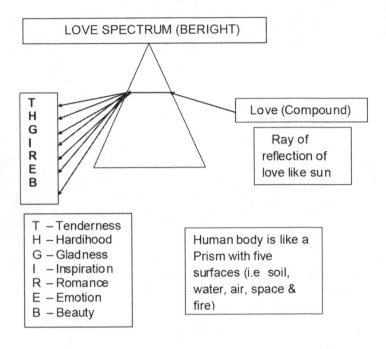

These seven colourful love lights activate in presence of eleven organs without which these seven colourful love lights-seem to be meaningless. On the one hand, these seven love rays are the main media to show their authority through their activities; on the other hand, these seven colourful rays become also worthless until the eleven organs play their vital roles individually. The whole system of the process comes to an end. How love has come in to being in our life in the midst of its each colourful ray flashed and illuminated by the activities of ten organs individually. If you take your broad outlook regarding both life and love, you must grasp that this body is transparent and smooth like a prism. Its smoothness and conspicuousness are developed because of love light from this example you will be able to fathom how 'love' permeates this human life. And under the authority of "love" how your life gets delighted and smiled just like the rising sun. Now let us treat of these seven colourful "love light" in their sequestered ways. And how the sense and active organs widen their essence coincided with them. According to the graph, it is obvious that these are seven colourful refracted rays of love like sun called 'love spectrum' (BE RIGHT) like solar spectrum (VIBGYOR) which have kept the inner world of life colourful and beautiful. In respect of these sacred colourful rays life looks exquisite and exhilarant, and seems to be cheerful freed from any sullenness. These colourful Rays of Love are displayed amid different activities of human being. These also get activated and manipulated by the organs of perception and the organs of action. Whenever this human body is conceived with Love Rays dispersed into seven colourful rays crowned with the best qualities humanity, where darkness of inhumanity is no longer, as the ray of the sun dispels the darkness and is dispersed into seven colourful rays in accordance with the test of spectrum occurred in the outside world. I hope the exploration of seven rays of love concerning life, "love spectrum", will make my readers realize the profound theme of love in life. So, it is obvious that you are obsessed with the light of love. Such attraction keeps you alive and life-like. In the absence of the light of love (i.e. seven colourful rays of love) your life will be void of the true nature of a proper human life apropos of "humanity". Without its presence the life is nothing but a mere life bereft of proper existence called humanity. So, the life seems to be non-existent being devoid of humanity. As a boy with the uniform of any school called a student merely, but if he is lacking of all qualities of studentship such as study and perseverance—he never becomes a real student in case of the true essence of a student. So, however, externally he is called a student, but internally he is nothing but another misguided boy. A piece of iron can be turned into a piece of magnet, but this piece of iron cannot be detected with your eyes whether it is a piece of magnet or not. So, with what power of the obsession of a piece magnet turned a piece of iron into a magnet is unseen and invisible. But it is the true essence and entity of a piece of iron from a piece of magnet. So, it is evident that what seems to be a true existence is unseen. Without enhancing the subtle knowledge of yourself it is quite impossible to grasp its mystery. On this point, I invite all to exhilarate your knowledge of humanity and try to get nuance what is love and what not.

Being a devotee of the truth if you shirk your main duty of discovering the true entity of yours, so, you are regarded as nothing but a malediction of human being. You are nothing but a transvestite to satisfy only your appetite for the gross body. What is the difference between your essence and beast like essence? So, without meandering comes closer to yours! You get initiated yourself with the subtle and sublime perception gifted by God and be a proper devotee of 'love' to hug a happy and beautiful life in your troublesome and complicated turn. Now I intend to discuss each colourful ray of love one after one reflecting through this prism like human body. Its presence is the essence of this beautiful life of which entity is your true beauty.

Ray of beauty: Now discussing that the first colourful ray of light of the love-like sun is the 'beauty'. In the field and in any case of love matter beauty must be the first and foremost matter. In the absence of beauty from both the inanimate and animate never be explainable and acceptable. Because every living being must be teemed with its own distinct beauty, without which it seems to be non-existent or spiritless; but this beauty may vary from man to man, even from any living being to another being. Always you have to think that 'beauty' is the life or main essence of any living being by itself, but here I have pointed to a human life. In this way the word 'beauty' can be thought as a collection of such qualities, they are shape, feature, colour, etc. pleasing and enjoying the aesthetic scenes, especially the sight. Here it is clear that beauty of anything first charms and attracts your 'sight'; your perceptible organ 'eye'. These perceptible organs activate every colourful ray of love-like sun. The 'eye' is the first sense organ of human body. Whenever your 'eye' is accustomed to judging any beauty of living being, it must enhance the profound latent knowledge of this expected subject (i.e. it may be both animate or inanimate) coming in contact the proper beauty, which may remain immanent and flourishing, that stands for truth, sanctity and real essence. Degree by degree, that beauty pleases the intellect or moral sense. So always you should remember that whenever the knowledge of your deep outlook of your 'eye' extends its scope, your attraction for that expected media must go on augmenting. Before I have told that such 'beauty' may vary from man to man. Suppose, to your eye a black-girl may be beautiful; but to the other it may be not; because you have found out the 'beauty' of that black-girl. In this respect, I intend to tell a few words through bringing out an example, such as—a bulb being covered with a blue-coloured paper, if a ray of light is reflected through it, you must find that this bulb must give blue light, because of its blue-paper covering. So, whatever the outside shape or feature or colour may be, it does not come into effect truly, the colourfully of 'beauty' always the same. It never changes its authentic colour. So, in order to judge the beauty of any being or thing never be understood by the outside colour or shape; it needs proper knowledge of the beauty of the expected subject with the help of your five organs of perception. Thus each perceptible organ must give you rays of knowledge by dint of which it may be able to judge the real beauty of your expected ones. So, you are requested to keep in mind that—whenever ray of love-like sun will be reflected into your mortal body, it must be turned into seven colourful rays collectively these seven colourful rays will dispel all darkness of ignorance and evil illusion from your life. Then your life will be inundated with the light of love. And the first colourful ray is 'beauty' of which influence, your body and mind will be engrossed and bathed in rays of beauty, where ugliness and darkness of untruth never exists. Since then other rays of love-like sun can display themselves conspicuously; and with this heart you can ask for love of others. And such 'beauty' is not a mere thing here. It goes on in its course. This 'beauty' activated by the perceptible organs, and by five organs of actions.

Whole matter depends on your mind, which is your internal super organ. it judges whether this beauty is acceptable or not.

Ray of Romance: 'Romance' can be explained in the words of the concise Oxford Lexicon; 1. An atmosphere or tendency characterized by a sense of remoteness from or idealization of everyday life; 2. A prevailing sense of wonder or mystery surrounding the mutual attraction of love affair; and sentimental or idealized love. It is evident that whenever 'beauty' is regarded as an acceptable matter, then 'romance' must come into being under the influence of 'beauty' that stands for Satyam, Sivam and Sundaram.Such elevating romance never gets wrong turn. In the midst of different qualities and characteristics of the 'beauty' of your expected media is activated by romance of the respective both perceptive and active organs. Such romance makes you so romantic in case of flourishing both your own beauty of knowledge and your expected one. Thus 'romance' gives you an immense fragrance of pleasure to forget all your suffering and frustration. In this way in your life, the path of love will be lighted gradually. Romance is a bit of thrilling of love-like sun that keeps both body and mind lighted in a romantic way.

Ray of emotion: Emotion is a kind of strong mental or instinctive feeling; and the part of a person's character that consists of feelings. Such emotional-ray lightens the world of affinity and inclination to the beauty. With the help of this ray of light man's inner longing for a specific beauty goes up. Regarding love, emotional attraction creates a feeling of thrilling for getting or for attachment with anything. Under the influence of the emotional affinity the perceptive and active organs get sharpened for the inner feeling. A kind of the beauty of anything (i.e. both animate and inanimate)—but here 'human being has been taken as a burning example).Whenever such emotion is infused into the human body, its all-prime constituents (i.e. ten organs & internal mind) engaged in different new creation accompanied by knowledge. Then by the light of such emotion a person's inner desire of characteristics become conscious. As a result, such a man becomes a suitable media for the displaying of love, and since then he is able to realize others' mental feeling with his strong instinctive feeling of emotion. In absence of such ray of emotion the true essence of love never be perceived clearly. If you see and think a little, it will be obvious to you that in respect of any relation with anyone a latent or an unuttered emotion is created, and it smoothly touches both sense and active organs of your body. But with the help of your subtle knowledge this emotion begins its creation, but whether it will be received or not wholly depends on the realization of the mind. All emotional latent organs rouse from the state of their sub consciousness. And having been lighted by true ray of emotion they respond to the inner unspoken call of the emotion of others. Then such emotion never expresses any corruption regarding love, because this emotion results from the co-existence of both consciousness and knowledge associated with emotional organs. Such emotion is not a strayed from the path of the truth, and this emotion begets a true prolonged pleasure, and love gets flourished through this emotion in the human life. Emotion is a sort of thrilling for creation and invention, which gives birth to a lot of ecstasies in life. Even it makes a man peep into Philosophy pertaining to both life and the world, because without emotion no life is lively and life-like. So emotionless life has not "motion" that means life. If your all organs seem emotionless instead of existing life, you are not a life-like. Both your knowledge and consciousness will remain latent and sleeping, so, in order to realize the reality and entity of love here emotion plays a fundamental role.

Ray of Tenderness (compassion): Love like sun also reflects ray of tenderness. Lacking of tenderness love can't be thought fully in life. On the point, compassion seems a compass to direct or guide the ship of humanity in the ocean of life regarding love. Love is a symbol of 'beauty which begets 'truth', "sanctity" and "purity" endowed with 'God' who stands for 'pity', 'sympathy', 'mercy', 'kindness', 'elementary', compassion and 'commiseration.' So a life, void of compassion, is not regarded as a true human life. Because 'humanity' is the crown of a human life; and this 'humanity' is a substitute for 'pity' and 'mercy' seemed tenderness. The ray of compassion drives away the darkness of harshness, discordance, and tartness from life. Without ray of compassion life will never be flourished, because 'humanity' faces an uttering disturbance to express itself in a full swing. Respecting this, the more you love, the more the ray of compassion will awaken your latent humanity (that is still covered with murkiness of curliness and sourness) from the state of the obscurity. With respect to this expected discussion, compassion is such one of the rays of love-like sun of which absence love is not fulfilled in the inner world of your life.

When a single colour is absent from the light of the sun, the outside world will never be lighted fully, because the sun is the main source of the light of the external world, for want of a single fragmentary colour the idea of the sun is not complete. So to get the warm and heavenly contact of love your life should be refreshed with seven colourful rays of love-like sun. Compassion is a beautiful passion of 'humanity', which begets pity. Hence 'humanity' and 'pity' are substitute for each other. Love never comes into being in a full-fledged without compassion. Compassion plays the key role to leave a deep impression of love upon life. Always you have to realize that seven rays of love-like sun are dependent on one another. In absence of one of them, others must be inactive, even life stops its spontaneous motion in the question of humanity, which is the first title for entrance of the royal gate of love in human life.

Ray of Hardihood (Patience): Patience is a great 'essence' of love. A life, which is free from patience, does not embrace love. Its role is very much indispensable relating to love and life. Where impatience there is is no spontaneous love. It is obvious that impatience is utterly contrary to patience; in the presence of impatience love can't express its ingredients properly in a life, so there love is not possible. Whenever love embraces life it is free from impatience facing a setback in the way of love. So, like other rays of love-like sun it (i.e. patience) it plays a vital role. As we know that patience is a great virtue; an impatient life is like a beast; because want of knowledge a beast generally is not able to show patience. So 'essence' of love can be realized beautifully in the life of colourful rays, which have kept lighted and lively the inner world of the life. To understand and feel the real countenance and nature of love these seven colourful rays are very indispensable. At every step of your life you must feel its necessity? Every part of your active life is chained with the invisible power of love; and every colourful ray of love is guiding you during the obscurity in your life. Otherwise you have to fall in the gall that gives birth to a dozen of bitterness, indignation and antipathy in your life; as a result you face it very hard and quandary to go ahead. So, to surmount all obstacles throughout your life, and to make your life smooth and pleasant you should yearn after the colourful ray of patience to imbue your perceptive organs to discern the reality of love from man to man. You have to remember that love is a 'hopeful-flower' hanging from the branch of life on the basis of the thought of eternity. So, if you long for the extreme pleasure of love you should try your best carefully and patiently to pluck up this 'hopeful-flower'. So, you should drive first away the darkness of impatience, and move patiently on to do succeed your expected wish, or to reach your lofty destination. Patience serves as a vigilant to observe love regarding life. To get any opportunity in course of life patience is a great 'pity' to rouse the entity of humanity respecting both life and love. With regard to this it can be expressed that— the more you will be patient, the more you will be successful in case of love. It is not possible for you to initiate the organs of perception through bathing with the ray of patience. You will never be able to walk along with

Ray of gladness: For want of the ray of pleasure every life would be sad and gloomy; and such a life is not active and spirited. Pleasure is the stream of spring that descends from the mountain of heaven along with the uneven path of the life having coincided with the fruit of the duty of your active life regarding love. Pleasure begets leisure amid love. So, you may think that pleasure is such a blessed flower gifted to and bestowed upon by God. Without pleasure life is bitter. Life is better where pleasure is. So it seems that the inner world of our life is always saturated with the unseen seven ecstatic-colourful rays of love. As a result your life seems or looks ecstatic and exhilarant. Colourless life never becomes happy and peaceful. So, the colour or hue of the mind is observed with mind's eye or inward eye. Hence, your eleven organs abstain from such colours, which stand for pleasure, so they gradually become inactive. If they don't get a little pleasure in their works how it is possible for them to carry on their duty. Regarding this pleasure is the pabulum to resuscitate your bereaved life. On the subject of the above discussion I request all of my readers to reflect the ray of love on the prism like body. Having dispersed into seven colourful rays of love and having dispelled all darkness these seven rays will lead you to the path of light.

TWENTYTWO CHAPTER

LOVE IS THE CENTRAL POINT OF MYSTICAL TRIANGLE

This book treats of different aspects to make its main theme easy so that my readers can realize easily what I have endeavoured to tell. Before closing the revised second edition I intend to introduce my readers to a new discussion. I hope it will be an influential and indispensable matter of thinking to all for on the basis of the distinct subject matter of 'A new philosophical classic: Theory of Love' I have made an effort my best to make it conspicuous. I shall request all of my readers to follow patiently and listen to what my facile pen is desire to speak of.

Love is the center of the triangle consisting of life, the world and philosophy without which nothing can be thought in a proper way regarding both the concrete and the abstract. It is obvious that our entrance with love and our exit with love to which the vast universe also inclined. In this chapter the very purport and singularity of love has been explicated through graph so that its real purpose is obvious. The stated at graph at the end of this chapter speaks of what love is really.

If you meticulously observe and consciously discern, it will be clear that nothing is complete without subtle presence of love. Is the universe existent without the thought of these three aspects? I am going to extend my discussion relating to the given graph infra.

Concerning the graph it is obvious that—whoever you may be? Or what class do you belong to? Or what type of profession do you hold? You are not out of these three categories. Your thinking, disposition, behavior and human characteristics etc must be in any of these three classes. If not, it will be assumed that you are not a denizen in this planet in the ken of human being. If everything is explained respecting life in case of the abstract and the concrete on the ground of philosophy so it will be convenient to understand clearly, because nothing is beyond the realization of philosophy. You are an idealist, or a naturalist, or a pragmatist because you are not out of this world, which is the best place to enliven these thoughts with regard to the life. Even this world is the thought of five phenomena consisting of soil, fire, and water. Space and air, and again these five elements cause a life though three invisible elements have been in case of human life. After all, life is the best media to realize these I have discussed in the previous chapters of this book. My readers, whatever you think or whatever you do is co-related with one another relating to this life and the world relying on philosophy. In the midst of the discussion respecting the life, world and philosophy love is the central point on which all these converged, where love sustains the life, world and philosophy as a prime source of power regarding the concrete and abstract.

Everywhere everyman is in an invisible chain of love. Love disposes every life to take such a path that leads him to the truth. Let us yearn for love, where god is nothing but a formal name. As long as the true entity of love exists in life, god exists in the identity of love in different ways in the individual belief according to the depth of knowledge. Love is a fine causal power of discrete reason felt by man amid various thoughts of idealism, naturalism and pragmatism. Nothing is beyond love. So let us live for love as to the abstract and than the concrete. Even from the minutest particle to the largest particle in this vast universe it is powerful loaded with the unseen power of love. It has been tried to elucidate the magnanimity of love through the mystic triangle.

In which way you will wish to analyze this universe concerning the life there mystical triangle must help you to explicate your unuttered thought; here love is the central point to construe the different sublimations relating to life. However little and broad thinking, it will come into effect, which stated the mystical triangle. Objectives of this mystical triangle are to pave the way for a special thought pertaining to love in case of universe. Though it may be multifarious accordingly individual concept, they are to be same to a distinct point of understanding. No thought of this universe turns into being without the contemplation of life, world and philosophy. I believe this mystical triangle will succour you enough to mitigate the tangle of mystery of love concerning life in this world.

Whatever we think is not out of the theme and outlook construed in the above mystical triangle. Hope this triangle will solve the tangle of mystery in life. Love is the purified power resulted from the mingling of life, world and philosophy; and of which underlying forces converged on it.

<u>The given graph divulges what mystical triangle speaks of the different ilks of Man (Male & Female)</u>

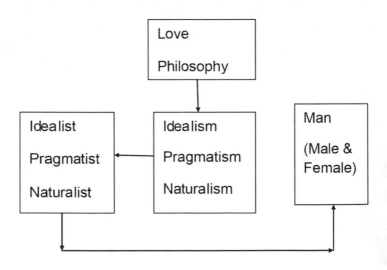

End